THE
ULTIMATE
QUESTION

THE ULTIMATE QUESTION

Driving Good Profits and True Growth

FRED REICHHELD

HARVARD BUSINESS SCHOOL PRESS
BOSTON, MASSACHUSETTS

978-1-59139-783-0 (ISBN 13)

Library of Congress Cataloging -in-Publication Data

Reichheld, Fred.
   The ultimate question : driving good profits and true growth / Fred Reichheld.
     p. cm.
   Includes index.
   ISBN 1-59139-783-9
   1. Customer relations. 2. Consumer satisfaction. 3. Customer loyalty.
4. Employee motivation. 5. Employee loyalty. 6. Leadership. 7. Success in
business. I. Title.
  HF5415.5.R439 2006
  658.15'54—dc22   2005025733

This book is dedicated to my wife, Karen,

with love and loyalty.

CONTENTS

PREFACE

This book shows how companies can put themselves on the path to true growth—growth that occurs because their customers love doing business with them and sing their praises to friends and colleagues.

This is the only kind of growth that can be sustained over the long term. Acquisitions, aggressive pricing strategies, product line extensions, new marketing campaigns, and all the other implements in a CEO's toolkit can give a company a short-term boost. But if these gambits don't ultimately result in delighted customers, the growth won't last. So it is with market share. A dominant position in the marketplace often gives a company economic advantage. But again: if that potential isn't utilized to make customers smile, neither the advantage nor the dominant share will last.

The real issue, however, isn't whether companies *should* delight their customers. Every chief executive and every manager wants customers to be happy with what they're getting. The real issue is how a company *knows* what its customers are feeling, and how it can establish *accountability* for the customer experience. Traditional satisfaction surveys just aren't up to this job. They ask too many questions and generate too little usable information. Financial reports aren't up to it, either. As we'll see, conventional accounting can't even distinguish a dollar of good profits—the kind that lead to growth—from a dollar of bad profits, which undermine it.

What the book offers instead is a wholly new kind of measurement, a measurement that can focus an entire organization on improving every customer's experience day in and day out. The process is both simple and radical. Companies need to ask just one question—the Ultimate Question—in a regular, systematic, and timely fashion. They need to track and publicize the answers, then they need to put the information to work right away. Just as managers now use financial reports to make sure they and their team members are meeting profit goals, they can use this new metric to make sure they are meeting customer-relationship goals. Therein lies the path to true growth.

The companies that have pioneered the use of this measurement—you will read about them in the chapters that follow—have already learned this lesson and are *way* out ahead of their competitors. They range from small neighborhood businesses to Silicon Valley superstars and giants such as General Electric. Different as they are in other respects, they have one big thing in common, which is that they take seriously the principle of the Golden Rule: treat others as you would want to be treated. These businesses want customers who are so pleased with how they are treated that they willingly come back for more and bring their friends and colleagues with them. Incidentally, though the book's examples are drawn from the business world, organizations of any kind—schools, hospitals, charities, even government agencies—can put these ideas to practical use as well. Nonbusiness organizations also have customers or constituents; they too need to delight the people they serve, and they too can benefit greatly from the use of one simple metric.

Once you have read the book, please visit the Web site www.netpromoter.com. My hope is that together we can create a community of people who believe that the purpose of companies and other organizations is to provide outstanding value and great relationships for their customers or members—and who think that an organization's best chance for long life and prosperity requires measuring performance on this dimension just as carefully as profits.

Part One

WHY THE ULTIMATE QUESTION WORKS

ONE

Bad Profits, Good Profits, and the Ultimate Question

Too many companies these days can't tell the difference between good profits and bad. As a result, they are getting hooked on bad profits.

The consequences are disastrous. Bad profits choke off a company's best opportunities for true growth, the kind of growth that is both profitable and sustainable. They blacken its reputation. The pursuit of bad profits alienates customers and demoralizes employees.

Bad profits also make a business vulnerable to competitors. Companies that are not addicted—yes, there are many—can and do zoom right past the bad-profits junkies. If you ever wondered how Enterprise Rent-A-Car was able to overcome big, well-entrenched companies to become number one in its industry, how Southwest Airlines and JetBlue Airways so easily steal market share from the old-line carriers, or how Vanguard soared to the top of the mutual fund industry, that's your answer. These companies just said no to bad profits, and their revenues and reputations have flourished.

The cost of bad profits extends well beyond a company's boundaries. Bad profits provide a distorted picture of business performance. The distortion misleads investors, yielding poor resource decisions that hurt our economy. Bad profits also tarnish the position of business in society. That tarnished reputation undermines consumer trust and provokes calls for stricter rules and tighter regulations. So long as companies pursue bad profits, all the noisy calls for better business ethics are so much hot air. The only way a company can truly live by the Golden Rule—treat others as you would like to be treated—is to avoid bad profits entirely.

By now you're probably wondering how in heaven's name *profit,* that holy grail of the business enterprise, can ever be bad. Short of outright fraud, isn't one dollar of earnings as good as another? Certainly, accountants can't tell the difference between good and bad profits. They all look the same on an income statement.

While bad profits don't show up on the books, they are easy to recognize. They're profits earned at the expense of customer relationships.

Whenever a customer feels misled, mistreated, ignored, or coerced, then profits from that customer are bad. Bad profits come from unfair or misleading pricing. Bad profits arise when companies save money by delivering a lousy customer experience. Bad profits are about extracting value from customers, not creating value. When sales reps push overpriced or inappropriate products onto trusting customers, the reps are generating bad profits. When complex pricing schemes dupe customers into paying more than necessary to meet their needs, those pricing schemes are contributing to bad profits.

You don't have to look far for examples. Financial services firms, for instance, like to throw around terms like *fiduciary* and *trust* in their advertising campaigns, but how many firms deserve these monikers? Mutual funds bury their often-exorbitant administrative fees in the fine print, so that customers won't know what they're paying. Brokerage firms slant their research to support investment-banking clients, thus bilking their stock-buying clients. Retail banks charge astonishing fees for late payments or bounced checks.

Or take health care. Too many hospitals won't reveal the deals they have cut with insurance companies. Too many insurers do their best to exclude people who might actually need coverage— and if you do have coverage, they're sure to drown both you and your doctor in a deluge of complicated paperwork. Many pharmaceutical companies pay doctors to push their drugs, while carefully quashing studies suggesting that a potentially lucrative new drug may be ineffective or dangerous. And many health-maintenance organizations promise to provide cradle-to-grave coverage, yet balk at paying for many procedures their own physicians recommend.

Travelers face their own set of inhospitable tactics. They must pay most airlines $100 to change a ticket and $80 for an extra piece of checked baggage. If they are so foolish as to use a hotel phone, they may find they have run up charges larger than the room rate. If they return most rental cars with less than a full tank, they will be charged more than triple the market price for the fill-up. Of course, they also have the option of buying a full tank at the beginning of the rental and then trying to manage their mileage so precisely that only fumes remain—they get no credit for unused gas.

At times, customers must conclude that businesspeople lie awake nights thinking up new ways to hustle them. Most airlines change their prices hundreds of times a day, so nobody can know what the "real" fare is. Banks develop algorithms that process the largest checks first each day, so that depositors will be hit with more insufficient-funds penalties. Many mobile-phone operators have created pricing plans that cleverly trap customers into wasting prepaid minutes or incurring outrageous overages.

Ironically, the best customers often get the worst deals. If you are a patient, loyal user of your telephone company, your mobile-phone provider, and your Internet-service company, chances are good that you are paying more than disloyal switchers who signed up more recently. In fact you're probably paying more than you need to, regardless of when you signed up, just because you didn't know about some special package the company offers. Customers who discover an extra charge of $20, say, for using text messaging find that unlimited text messaging is available for $5 per month— if only they had asked for it in advance.

HOW BAD PROFITS UNDERMINE GROWTH

Bad profits work much of their damage through the *detractors* they produce. Detractors are customers who feel badly treated by a company—so badly that they cut back on their purchases, switch to the competition if they can, and warn others to stay away from the company they feel has done them wrong.

Detractors don't show up on any organization's balance sheet, but they cost a company far more than most of the liabilities that traditional accounting methods so carefully tally. Customers who feel ignored or mistreated find ways to get even. They drive up service costs by reporting numerous problems. They demoralize frontline employees with their complaints and demands. They gripe to friends, relatives, colleagues, acquaintances—anyone who will listen, sometimes including journalists, regulators, and legislators. Detractors tarnish a firm's reputation and diminish its ability to recruit the best employees and customers. Today, negative word of mouth goes out over a global PA system. In the past, the accepted maxim was that every unhappy customer told ten friends. Now an unhappy customer can tell ten thousand "friends" through the Internet.

Bad profits—and the detractors they create—strangle a company's growth. If many of your customers are bad-mouthing you, how are you going to get more? If many of your customers feel mistreated, how can you persuade them to buy more from you? Right now, churn rates in many industries—cellular phones, credit cards, newspapers, and cable TV—have deteriorated to the point where a typical company loses half of its new customers in less than three years. Many airlines have created so much ill will that customers are itching for an alternative. For a while, US Airways dominated the Philadelphia market. The company's fares were high and its service mediocre, but the routes into and out of Philadelphia were highly profitable. Then Southwest Airlines entered the market with lower fares. US Airways dropped its prices to match Southwest's, but travelers flocked to the new carrier anyway—they had had enough.

True growth is hard to find these days. How hard? A recent study by Bain & Company found that only 22 percent of the world's major firms achieved real, sustainable growth of even 5 percent a year over the ten-year period from 1994 to 2004.[1] It seems like no coincidence that so many companies are having trouble growing and so many companies are addicted to bad profits. To change metaphors, business leaders have become master mechanics in siphoning out current earnings, but they fumble for the right wrench when it comes to gearing up for growth.

Granted, companies can always buy growth. They can encourage the hard sell and pay fat commissions to the salespeople who master it. They can discount heavily, offering temporary rebates, sales, or "free" financing. They can launch heavy advertising and promotional campaigns. And of course they can make acquisitions.

All such techniques may boost revenues, but only for a while. Consider the sorry experience of America Online, which launched a successful initial public offering in March 1992 and might have invested its new cash in service and quality enhancements. Instead, AOL opted to buy growth by carpet-bombing the country with free software diskettes. You could find the diskettes tucked into the pages of magazines, packaged with your in-flight snacks on airplane trips, and displayed at the checkout stands of all kinds of stores. The campaign was apparently successful—AOL's membership grew rapidly—but the flood of new users began to strain the capacity of the company's operating network. AOL earned a new nickname, "America On Hold," and created an army of detractors. A full-day blackout in the summer of 1996—the largest in a series of service interruptions around this time, as it turned out—made headlines across the country and frustrated millions of members. AOL's monthly customer churn rate rose to 6 percent (an annual rate of 72 percent!). Searching for a way to boost current earnings, management turned to advertising revenues; AOL then began to inundate customers with pop-up ads and sales pitches. But as the company's membership surged to a peak of 35 million, detractors began to choke off its growth.

By 2002, surveys showed that a whopping 42 percent of AOL's customers were detractors. AOL not only lost customers to broadband, it also lost market share to dial-up competitors MSN and Earthlink, and even today it is still trying to restore its damaged reputation through advertising and "bribing" customers with special promotional deals. As it shifts strategy to become a free content provider (more like Yahoo! and Google), with much of its support provided by advertisers, its chances for success will be seriously compromised by its millions of vociferous detractors. "Long ago," wrote Randall Stross of the *New York Times* in late 2005, "the company's culture became accustomed to concentrating energy on trapping customers who wished to leave."[2]

So it is with too many other companies. Buying growth is expensive. It tends to create a profit squeeze, which in turn usually deepens a company's addiction to bad profits. Retail banks, for example, now depend on nuisance fees for as much as one-third of reported earnings. One mobile-phone operator calculates that proactively putting customers in the plan that was best for them would cut profits by 40 percent. This addiction to bad profits demotivates employees, diminishes the chances for true growth, and accelerates a destructive spiral. Customers resent bad profits—but investors should, too, because bad profits undermine a company's prospects. Like the addicts they are, enterprises dependent on bad profits have no future until they can break their habit.

THE ALTERNATIVE: GOOD PROFITS

But it doesn't have to be this way. Some companies grow because they have learned to tell the difference between bad profits and good profits—and to focus their efforts on the good kind.

Good profits are dramatically different. If bad profits are earned at the expense of customers, good profits are earned with customers' enthusiastic cooperation. A company earns good profits when it so delights its customers that they willingly come back for more—and not only that, they tell their friends and colleagues to do business with the company. Satisfied customers become, in effect, part of the company's marketing department, not only increasing their own purchases but also providing enthusiastic referrals. They become *promoters.* The right goal for a company that wants to break the addiction to bad profits is to build relationships of such high quality that those relationships create promoters, generate good profits, and fuel growth.

The Vanguard Group of mutual funds offers a compelling illustration of the difference between bad profits and good. Not long ago, Vanguard *reduced* prices by as much as one-third for customers who had recently made large investments or who had maintained healthy balances for an extended period. Vanguard's management recognized that the company had inadvertently been overcharging its best customers and (in essence) subsidizing new customers. To many companies, that might seem like a smart way to grow. To Vanguard, not only were those bad profits unethical, they didn't make good business sense. When the company righted the wrong, its core customers were so delighted that they increased their holdings and boosted referrals. That helped turbocharge Vanguard's growth, and pushed the company toward leadership in the mutual funds industry. Nor is Vanguard alone in its pursuit of good profits. For example:

> Amazon.com could easily afford to advertise more than it does; instead it channels its investments into free shipping, lower prices, and service enhancements. Founder and CEO Jeff Bezos has said, "If you do build a great experience, customers tell each other about that."[3]

> Southwest Airlines doesn't charge for flight changes, instead offering passengers a credit that can be used anytime over the

next twelve months; the carrier has also replaced the industry's elaborate segmented pricing structure with a transparent two-tier pricing policy. Southwest now flies more domestic passengers than any other U.S. airline and boasts a market capitalization greater than the rest of the industry combined.

Costco, the leader in customer loyalty among warehouse retailers, has rocketed from start-up to the *Fortune* 50 in less than twenty years while spending next to nothing on advertising and marketing. Its customers are so loyal that the company can rely on positive word of mouth for its growth.

Even in a business as mature as insurance, Northwestern Mutual has used its 5 percentage point customer-retention advantage to overtake the leviathans as the number one issuer of individual life policies.

Among Internet companies, the astonishing growth of eBay stands in remarkable contrast to the stalled growth of AOL. The eBay Web site says this:

eBay is a community that encourages open and honest communication among all its members. Our community is guided by five fundamental values:

- *We believe people are basically good.*

- *We believe everyone has something to contribute.*

- *We believe that an honest, open environment can bring out the best in people.*

- *We recognize and respect everyone as a unique individual.*

- *We encourage you to treat others the way you want to be treated.*[4]

eBay is firmly committed to these principles. And we believe that community members should also honor them—whether buying, selling, or chatting with eBay friends.

Of course, anyone can list high-minded principles on a Web site or a recruiting brochure. But eBay has found ways to translate these principles into daily priorities and decisions. The result is that more than 70 percent of eBay customers are promoters and have remained so even after the company's controversial price increases of early 2005. Referrals generate more than half of the site's new customers, creating multiple economic advantages across the business. Like Costco, eBay relies more on word of mouth than on advertising and traditional marketing. The company has found that referred customers cost less to serve because they've already been coached by a promoter on how the site works and they usually have friends who help solve their problems instead of relying on eBay employees. EBay has also learned to tap the creativity of an entire online community, not just its own employees. The company encourages members to point out areas in which they believe eBay isn't living up to its principles, and to identify new opportunities to better serve members. Community members are invited to rate each other after each transaction, and the ratings are then shared with everybody. This process enables each member to establish a reputation based not on public relations or advertising spin but on the cumulative experience of members with whom they've done business. EBay's virtual world is just like a small town: a good name is essential for success.

Conventional wisdom encourages companies to consolidate market power and then extract maximum value from customers. Yet eBay has done just the opposite. Although it has come to dominate the online auction market, the company tries to consider the needs of community members as well as the long-term interests of its shareholders when it makes decisions. Running a company like a community enables eBay to look beyond the next quarter's stock price and to continually find ways to enrich the lives of community members. For example, the company created a group health insurance plan for its so-called PowerSellers—typically small merchants—who don't have access to the scale economies of corporate health plans. Although eBay facilitates the program, it doesn't take a profit margin.

Moves like this demonstrate a way of thinking that is radically different from the thinking of bad-profits companies. The airlines have repeatedly used their market power to raise prices, sometimes to levels that can only be described as price gouging. AOL alienated customers not just with those service failures and pop-up ads, but also by continuing to charge for minutes used and resisting a move to flat monthly fees. EBay could easily increase profits by boosting ad revenue—but management recognizes that doing so would make the site less valuable to community members and possibly put small merchants at a disadvantage relative to large players.

This way of thinking also demonstrates a deep respect for the power of word of mouth in today's economy. Just as detractors have a bullhorn for spreading their negative word of mouth, promoters have one for spreading their positive word of mouth. Promoters bring in new people. They talk up a company and burnish its reputation. They extend the company's sales force at no cost. They make it possible for a company to earn good profits and thereby to create growth that is both profitable and sustainable. Again, that's what we mean by *true* growth.

This approach to customers boils down to a simple precept: treat them the way you would like to be treated. What's surprising is that so many company leaders articulate it in exactly these homespun terms. EBay founder Pierre Omidyar literally says, "My mother always taught me to treat other people the way I want to be treated and to have respect for other people."[5] Other leaders invoke the Golden Rule as well:

> Colleen Barrett, president of Southwest Airlines: "Practicing the Golden Rule is integral to everything we do."

> Isadore Sharp, founder and CEO of the Four Seasons hotel group: "Our success all boils down to following the Golden Rule."

> Andy Taylor, CEO of Enterprise Rent-A-Car: "The only way to grow is to treat customers so well they come back for more, and tell their friends about us. That's how we'd all like to be treated as customers." Taylor concluded, "Golden Rule behavior is the basis for loyalty. And loyalty is the key to profitable growth."

BAD AND GOOD PROFITS: HOW CAN COMPANIES TELL THE DIFFERENCE?

Loyalty is the key to profitable growth. That makes sense as far as it goes. But it raises as many questions as it answers. Most companies can't even define loyalty, let alone measure and manage it. Are customers sticking around out of loyalty, or just out of ignorance and inertia? Are they trapped in long-term contracts they would love to get out of? Anyway, how can managers really know how many of their customers love the company and how many hate it? What practical gauge can distinguish good profits from bad?

Without a systematic feedback mechanism, after all, the Golden Rule is self-referential and simplistic, unreliable for decision making. I might think I'm treating you the way I would like to be treated, but you may strongly disagree. Where companies are concerned, satisfaction surveys often delude executives into thinking that their performance merits an A, while their customers are thinking C– or F. Business leaders need a hard, no-nonsense metric—an honest grading system—that tells them how they are *really* doing.

The search for that metric—the missing link between the Golden Rule, loyalty, and true growth—turned out to be a long and arduous quest.

Together with my colleagues at Bain & Company, I began investigating the connection between loyalty and growth almost twenty-five years ago. We first compiled data demonstrating that a 5 percent increase in customer retention could yield anywhere from a 25 percent to a 100 percent improvement in profits. Later, we showed that companies with the highest customer loyalty (we labeled them *loyalty leaders*) typically grew revenues at more than twice the rate of their competitors.

Of course, not everybody was eager to learn about the mysterious *loyalty effect,* which explained how building relationships worthy of loyalty translated into superior profits and growth. The corporate generals at places like Enron, Tyco, and Adelphia couldn't have cared less about treating customers right. But the vast majority of senior executives seemed to buy into the concept. After all, it doesn't take a rocket scientist to see that a company can't grow if it is churning customers out the back door faster than the sales force can drag them in the front.

Still, there's a puzzle lurking here. Survey after survey demonstrates that customer loyalty *is* among most CEOs' top priorities—yet the colonels, captains, and corporals in their organizations continue to treat customers in ways that ensure these customers won't be coming back anytime soon. If the CEOs are as powerful as they are said to be, why can't they make their employees care about customer relationships?

The reason, of course, is just what I alluded to earlier in this chapter: employees are held accountable for increasing profits. Financial results are what companies measure. Financial results determine how managers fare in their performance reviews. Trouble is, accounting procedures can't distinguish a dollar of good profits from a dollar of bad. Did that $10 million in incremental profit come from new hidden surcharges, or did it come from loyal customers' repeat purchases? Did that $5 million in cost reduction come from shaving service levels, or from cutting customer defection rates? Who knows the answer to any such question? And if nobody knows, who cares? Managers trying to run a department or division can't be faulted for paying attention to the metrics by which they will be judged.

Whatever the CEO might think, in short, companies that measure success primarily through the lens of financial accounting tend to conclude that loyalty is dead, relationships are irrelevant, and the treatment of customers should be governed by what seems profitable rather than by what seems right. With only financial metrics to gauge success, managers focus on profits regardless of whether those profits represent the rewards from building relationships or the spoils from abusing them. Ironically, customer loyalty provides companies with a powerful financial advantage— a battalion of credible sales and marketing and PR troops who require no salary or commissions. Yet the importance of these customer promoters is overlooked because they don't show up on anybody's income statement or balance sheet.

Finally, at a European conference on loyalty, one of my colleagues provided a crucial insight into this conundrum. Watching the executives file out of the room after a presentation, seemingly pumped up about loyalty as never before, he shook his head. "You know, it's sad," he said. "Right now, they all understand that their businesses can't prosper without improving customer loyalty. But they'll get back to their offices and soon recognize that there is no one in their organization to whom they can delegate the task. There is no system to help them measure loyalty in a way that makes individuals accountable for results."

Bingo. *Accountability* is one of those magic words in business. Any experienced manager will tell you that where there is individual accountability, things get done. *Measure* is another magic word: what gets measured *creates* accountability. With no standard, reliable metric for customer relationships, employees can't be held accountable for them and so overlook their importance. In contrast, the precise, rigorous, daily measures of profit and its components ensure that those same employees—at least the ones who wish to stay employed—feel personally accountable for costs, revenues, or both. So the pursuit of profit dominates corporate and individual agendas, while accountability for building good relationships gets lost in the shadows.

Several years ago, we thought we had solved this measurement challenge. We had helped companies develop a whole set of key measures such as retention rate, repurchase rate, and "share of wallet." But then we had to face reality. Most organizations found it difficult to collect accurate and timely data on these loyalty metrics. The companies were simply unable to rebalance their priorities and establish accountability for building good relationships with customers. Though the science of measuring profits had progressed steadily since the advent of double-entry bookkeeping in the fifteenth century, measuring the quality of relationships remained stuck in the dark ages, trapped by the pseudoscience of satisfaction surveys. Companies lacked a practical, operational system for gauging the percentage of their customer relationships that were growing stronger and the percentage that were growing weaker—and for getting the right employees to take appropriate actions based on this data.

So we went back to the drawing board. What we needed was a foolproof test—a practical metric for relationship loyalty that would illuminate the difference between good profits and bad. We had to find a metric that would permit individual accountability. We knew that the fleeting attitudes expressed in satisfaction surveys couldn't define loyalty; only actual behaviors can gauge loyalty and can fuel growth. So we concluded that behaviors must be the real building blocks. We needed a metric based on what customers would actually do.

After considerable research and experimentation, some of which you'll read about in the following chapters, we found one such metric. We discovered the one question you can ask your customers that links so closely to their behaviors that it is a practical surrogate for what they will do. By asking that question systematically, and by linking results to employee rewards, you can tell the difference between good profits and bad. You can manage for customer loyalty and the growth it produces just as rigorously as you now manage for profits.

Customer responses to this question yield a simple, straightforward measurement. This simple, easy-to-collect metric can make your employees accountable for treating customers right. It's one number you need to grow. That's why we call the question that produces it the Ultimate Question: this question will determine the future of your business.

ASKING THE ULTIMATE QUESTION

What is the question that can tell good profits from bad? Simplicity itself: How likely is it that you would recommend this company to a friend or colleague? The metric that it produces is the *Net Promoter® Score.**

Net Promoter Score (NPS) is based on the fundamental perspective that every company's customers can be divided into three categories. *Promoters,* as we have seen, are loyal enthusiasts who keep buying from a company and urge their friends to do the same. *Passives* are satisfied but unenthusiastic customers who can be easily wooed by the competition. And *detractors* are unhappy customers trapped in a bad relationship. Customers can be categorized according to their answer to the question. Those who answer nine or ten on a zero-to-ten scale, for instance, are promoters, and so on down the line.

A "growth engine" running at perfect efficiency would convert 100 percent of a company's customers into promoters. The worst possible engine would convert 100 percent into detractors. The best way to gauge the efficiency of the growth engine is to take the percentage of customers who are promoters (P) and subtract the percentage who are detractors (D). This equation is how we calculate a company's NPS:

$$P - D = NPS$$

In concept, it's just that simple. All the complexity arises from learning how to ask the question in a manner that provides reliable, timely, and actionable data—and, of course, from learning how to improve your NPS.

How do companies stack up on this measurement? Those with the most efficient growth engines—companies such as Amazon.com, eBay, Costco, Vanguard, and Dell—operate at NPS

---

* Ownership of this trademarked term will be shared by Satmetrix Systems, Inc., Bain & Company, and myself. Our goals are to encourage universal and consistent usage of NPS and to protect against its misappropriation.

efficiency ratings of about 50 to 80 percent (exhibit 1-1). So even they have room for improvement. But the average firm sputters along at an NPS efficiency of only 5 to 10 percent. In other words, promoters barely outnumber detractors. Many firms—and some entire industries—have *negative* Net Promoter Scores, which means that they are creating more detractors than promoters day in and day out. These abysmal scores explain why so many companies can't deliver profitable, sustainable growth, no matter how aggressively they spend to acquire new business.

EXHIBIT 1-1

Selected NPS stars

USAA	82%
HomeBanc*	81%
Harley-Davidson	81%
Costco	79%
Amazon.com	73%
Chick-fil-A*	72%
eBay	71%
Vanguard	70%
SAS	66%
Apple	66%
Intuit (TurboTax)*	58%
Cisco	57%
FedEx	56%
Southwest Airlines	51%
American Express	50%
Commerce Bank	50%
Dell	50%
Adobe	48%
Electronic Arts	48%

*All NPS statistics are based on Bain or Satmetrix surveys, with the exceptions of Intuit, Chick-fil-A, and HomeBanc. For these firms, we used data that they provided. Their data was gathered in a reasonable (but not perfectly equivalent) fashion.

Our research over a ten-year period confirms that, in most industries, companies with the highest ratio of promoters to detractors in their sector typically enjoy both strong profits and healthy growth. This might seem counterintuitive. After all, the high-loyalty firms tend to spend much less on marketing and new-customer acquisition than do their competitors. They also focus intensely on serving existing customers and are highly selective in pursuing new customers, which you might suspect would limit these firms' growth. But the data doesn't lie: the faster growth of the loyalty leaders is driven by the superior efficiency of their growth engines. Earning growth rather than buying it sustains top-line momentum while generating richer profits.

Most business leaders desperately need growth. They need it to boost their stock price. They need it to attract and motivate talent. Whatever language they may use, they probably know that creating more customer promoters is vital. But without a simple, practical way to assign accountability and measure progress, they can't align their organizations around this goal. Indeed, most don't realize how deeply addicted to bad profits they have become. Inflated customer-satisfaction scores have lulled them into complacency— yet our research shows that for the average firm, more than two-thirds of customers are passives (bored) or detractors (angry). Given this sad fact, most attempts to buy growth simply burn up shareholder funds. The efforts amount to throwing money into advertising and sales only to dissipate the impact through the poisonous emissions of unhappy customers.

HOW THE BOOK ADDRESSES THE ULTIMATE QUESTION

So here's what you'll find in the pages that follow. The first part of this book explains how Net Promoter Scores work to distinguish bad profits from good profits and to illuminate the path to true growth. This section shows you how to calculate your own NPS and benchmark your performance against world-class standards. Part 2 explains how to avoid the pitfalls of customer-satisfaction surveys and construct a practical measurement process that can turn NPS into a reliable tool for assigning accountability and managing priorities. The final part illustrates how leading companies are using this approach to provide a better customer experience and thus build better relationships with their customers. It lays out the steps you should follow to improve your customer relationships and turbocharge your growth.

Bad profits have undermined true growth and have given business a bad name. But it's not too late to change. Some companies have already begun.

TWO

The Measure of Success

Scott Cook was worried. His financial-software company, Intuit, was on a slippery slope, and he wasn't sure what to do about it.

Granted, his problems might not have looked overwhelming to an outsider. Intuit had grown like gangbusters ever since its birth in 1983. Its three major products—Quicken, QuickBooks, and TurboTax—dominated their markets. The company had gone public in 1993, and by the end of the decade was racking up sizable profits. Intuit had also been lauded by the business press as an icon of customer service, and Cook—a mild-mannered, bespectacled Harvard MBA who had done a stint at Procter & Gamble before cofounding the company—had a gut-level grasp of the importance of customer promoters. "We have hundreds of thousands of salespeople," he told *Inc.* magazine as early as 1991. "They're our customers." Intuit's mission? "To make the customer feel so good about the product they'll go and tell five friends to buy it."

But now—was that really happening? Cook wasn't sure. When the company was in its start-up phase, operating out of cozy offices in Silicon Valley, he had known every employee personally, and he could coach them all on the importance of making products and delivering services that customers truly loved. They could all hear him working the service phones himself, talking to customers. They could see him taking part in Intuit's famous "follow-me-home" program, where employees asked customers if they could watch them set up the software in order to note any problems. But now the company had thousands of people in multiple locations. Like many rapidly growing businesses, it had hired a lot of professional managers, who had been trained to run things by the numbers.

And what were those numbers? There were two requirements for growth, Cook liked to say: *profitable* customers and *happy* customers. Everyone knew how to measure profits, but the only measurements of customers' happiness were vague statistics of "satisfaction"—statistics derived from surveys that nobody trusted and nobody was accountable for.

So managers naturally focused on profits, with predictable consequences. The executive who cut staffing levels in the phone-support queue to reduce costs wasn't held accountable for the increased hold times or the resulting customer frustration. The phone rep who so angered a longtime customer that he switched to another tax-software product could still receive a quarterly bonus, because she handled so many calls per hour. Her batting average on productivity was easy to measure, but her batting average on customer good will was invisible. The marketing manager who kept approving glitzy new features to attract more customers was rewarded for boosting revenues and profits, when in fact the added complexity created a bewildering maze that turned off new users. Now, Cook was hearing more complaints than in the past. Some market-share numbers were slipping. For lack of a good system of measurement—and for lack of the accountability that accurate measurement creates—the company seemed to be losing sight of exactly what had made it great: its relationships with its customers.

THE CHALLENGE: MEASURING CUSTOMER HAPPINESS

In a way, Cook's experience recapitulated business history. Back in the days when every business was a small business, a proprietor could *know w*hat his customers were thinking and feeling. He knew them personally. He could see with his own eyes what made them happy and what made them mad. Customer feedback was immediate and direct—and if he wanted to stay in business, he paid attention to it.

But soon companies were growing too big for their owners or managers to know every customer. Individual customers came and went; the tide of customers ebbed and flowed. Without the ability to gauge what people were thinking and feeling, corporate managers naturally focused on how much those customers were spending, a number that was easily measurable. If our revenue is growing and we're making money, so the thinking ran, we must be doing something right.

Later, of course—and particularly after the arrival of powerful computers—companies tried to assess customers' attitudes more directly. They hired market-research firms to conduct satisfaction surveys. They tried to track customer-retention rates. These endeavors were so fraught with difficulties that managers outside marketing departments generally, and wisely, ignored the efforts. Retention rates, for example, track customer defections—how fast the customer bucket is emptying—but say nothing on the equally important question of how fast the bucket is filling up. They are a particularly poor indication of attitudes whenever customers are held hostage by high switching costs or other barriers. (Think of those US Airways Philadelphia travelers before Southwest Airlines arrived on the scene.)

Conventional customer-satisfaction measures are even less reliable. We will review their legendary shortcomings in detail later in the book (chapter 5). For the moment, it's enough to note that there is little connection between satisfaction rates and actual customer behavior, or between satisfaction rates and a company's growth. That's why investors typically ignore reports on customer satisfaction. In some cases, indeed, the relationship between satisfaction and performance is exactly backward. In the spring of 2005, for example, General Motors was taking out full-page newspaper ads trumpeting its numerous awards from J.D. Power and Associates, the biggest name in satisfaction studies. Meanwhile, the headlines in the business section were announcing that GM's market share was sinking and its bonds were being downgraded to junk status.

So as my colleagues and I continued our study of loyalty, we searched for a better measure—a simple and practical indicator of what customers were thinking and feeling about the companies they did business with. We wanted a number that reliably linked these attitudes to what customers actually did, and to the growth of the company in question.

What a chore it turned out to be! We started with the roughly twenty questions on the Loyalty Acid Test, a survey Bain designed several years ago to assess the state of relations between a company and its customers. (Sample questions: How likely are you to continue buying Company X's products or services? How would you rate the overall quality of the products and services provided by

Company X?) Then we sought the assistance of Satmetrix Systems, Inc., a company that develops software to gather and analyze real-time customer feedback. (Full disclosure: I serve on Satmetrix's board of directors.)

With Satmetrix, we administered the test to thousands of customers recruited from public lists in six industries: financial services, cable and telecommunications, personal computers, e-commerce, auto insurance, and Internet service providers. We obtained a purchase history for every person surveyed. We also asked these people to name specific instances when they had referred someone else to the company in question. When this information wasn't immediately available, we waited six to twelve months and then gathered information on subsequent purchases and referrals by those individuals. Eventually we had detailed information from more than four thousand customers, and we were able to build fourteen case studies—that is, cases for which we had sufficient sample sizes to measure the link between individual customers' survey responses and those same individuals' purchase or referral behavior.

DISCOVERING THE ULTIMATE QUESTION

All this number crunching had one goal: to determine which survey questions showed the strongest statistical correlation with repeat purchases or referrals. We hoped to find for each industry at least one question that effectively predicted what customers would do and hence helped predict a company's growth. We took bets on what the question would be. My own favorite—probably reflecting my years of research on loyalty—was, "How strongly do you agree that Company X deserves your loyalty?"

But what we found was different, and it surprised us all. It turned out that one question—the Ultimate Question—worked best for *most* industries. And that question was, "How likely is it that you would recommend Company X to a friend or colleague?" In eleven of the fourteen cases, this question ranked first or second. In two of the three others, it was so close to the top that it could serve as a proxy for those that did rank number one or number two.

Reflecting on our findings, we realized they made perfect sense. Loyalty, after all, is a strong and value-laden concept, usually applied to family, friends, and country. People may *be* loyal to a company that they buy from, but they may not describe what they feel in those terms. If they really love doing business with a particular provider of goods or services, however, what's the most natural thing for them to do? Of course: recommend that company to someone they care about.

We also realized that two conditions must be satisfied before customers make a personal referral. They must believe that the company offers superior value in terms that an economist would understand: price, features, quality, functionality, ease of use, and all the other practical factors. But they also must *feel* good about their relationship with the company. They must believe the company knows and understands them, values them, listens to them, and shares their principles. On the first dimension, a company is engaging the customer's head. On the second, it is engaging the heart. Only when both sides of the equation are fulfilled will a customer enthusiastically recommend a company to a friend. The customer must believe that the friend will get good value—but he or she also must believe that the company will treat the friend right. That's why the "would recommend" question provides such an effective measure of relationship quality. It tests for both the rational and the emotional dimensions.

I don't want to overstate the case. Though the "would recommend" question is far and away the best predictor of customer behavior across a range of industries, it's not the best for every industry. In certain business-to-business settings, a question such as "How likely is it that you will continue to purchase products or services from Company X?" may be better. So companies need to do their homework. They need to validate the link between survey answers and behavior for their own business and their own customers. But once some such link is established, as we will see in chapter 3, the results are incredibly powerful: it provides the means for gauging performance, establishing accountability, and making investments. It provides a connection to growth.

SCORING THE ANSWERS

Of course, finding the right question to ask was only the beginning. We now had to establish a good way of scoring the responses.

This may seem like a trivial problem, but any statistician knows that it isn't. To be useful, the scoring of responses must be as simple and unambiguous as the question itself. The scale must make sense to customers who are answering the question. The categorization of answers must make sense to the managers and employees responsible for interpreting the results and taking action. The right categorization will effectively divide customers into groups that deserve different attention and different responses from the company. Ideally, the scale and categorization would be so easy to understand that even outsiders—investors, regulators, journalists—could grasp the basic messages without the need for a handbook and a course in statistics.

For these reasons we settled on a simple zero-to-ten scale, where ten means "extremely likely" to recommend, five is neutral, and zero means "not at all likely." When we mapped customers' behaviors on this scale, we found three logical clusters (exhibit 2-1):

- One segment was the customers who gave a company a nine or ten rating. We called them *promoters,* because they behaved like promoters. They reported the highest repurchase rates by far, and they accounted for more than 80 percent of referrals.

- A second segment was the "passively satisfied" or *passives;* they rated the company seven or eight. This group's repurchase and referral rates were a lot lower than those of promoters, often by 50 percent or more. Motivated more by inertia than by loyalty or enthusiasm, these customers may not defect—until somebody offers them a better deal.

- Finally, we called the group who gave ratings from zero to six *detractors.* This group accounts for more than 80 percent of negative word-of-mouth comments. Some of these customers may appear profitable from an accounting standpoint, but their criticisms and attitudes diminish a company's reputation, discourage new customers, and demotivate employees. They suck the life out of a firm.

Grouping customers into these three clusters—promoters, passives, and detractors—provides a simple, intuitive scheme that accurately predicts customer behavior. Most important, it's a scheme that can be acted upon. Frontline managers can grasp the idea of increasing the number of promoters and reducing the number of detractors a lot more readily than the idea of raising the customer-satisfaction index by one standard deviation. The ultimate test for any customer-relationship metric is whether it helps the organization tune its growth engine to operate at peak efficiency. Does it help employees clarify and simplify the job of

EXHIBIT 2-1

Mapping responses to the ultimate question

"How likely is it that you would recommend
Company X to a friend or colleague?"

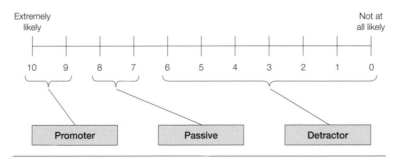

delighting customers? Does it allow employees to compare their performance from week to week and month to month? The notion of promoters, passives, and detractors does all this.

We also found that what we began to call *Net Promoter Score* (NPS)—the percentage of promoters minus the percentage of detractors—provided the easiest-to-understand, most effective summary of how a company was performing in this context.

We didn't come to this language or this precise metric lightly. For example, we considered referring to the group scoring a company nine or ten as "delighted," in keeping with the aspiration of so many companies to delight their customers. But the business goal here isn't merely to delight customers; it's to turn them into promoters—customers who buy more and who actively refer friends and colleagues. That's the behavior that contributes to growth. We also wrestled with the idea of keeping it even simpler—measuring only the percentage of customers who are promoters. But as we'll see in later chapters, a company seeking growth must increase the percentage of promoters *and* decrease the percentage of detractors. These are two distinct processes that are best managed separately. Companies that must serve a wide variety of customers in addition to their targeted core—retailers, banks, airlines, and so on—need to minimize detractors among noncore customers, since these customers' negative word of mouth is just as destructive as anybody's. But investing to delight customers other than those in the core rarely makes economic sense. Net Promoter Scores provide the requisite information for fine-tuning customer management in this way.

Individual customers, of course, can't have an NPS; they can only be promoters, passives, or detractors. But companies can calculate their Net Promoter Scores for particular segments of customers, for divisions or geographic regions, and for individual branches or stores. NPS is to customer relationships what a company's net profit is to financial performance. It's the one number that really matters—which is just what Intuit discovered.

SOLVING INTUIT'S PROBLEM

Intuit—worried as it was about slipping customer relationships—jumped at the idea of measuring its NPS and began an implementation program in the spring of 2003. ("Just one number—it makes so much sense!" exclaimed Scott Cook when he learned of the idea.) The company's experience shows some of what's involved in measuring promoters and detractors. It also shows how this measurement can transform a company's day-to-day priorities.

Intuit's first step was to determine the existing mix of promoters, passives, and detractors in each major business line. Cook suggested that this initial phone-survey process focus on only two questions. The team settled on these: first, What is the likelihood you would recommend (TurboTax, for example) to a friend or colleague? and second, What is the most important reason for the score you gave?

Customer responses revealed initial Net Promoter Scores for Intuit's business lines ranging from 27 to 52 percent. That wasn't bad, given that the average U.S. company has an NPS of less than 10 percent, but Intuit has never been interested in being average. The scores weren't consistent with the company's self-image as a firm that values doing right by its customers. The numbers convinced the management team that there was plenty of room for improvement.

The initial audit revealed something else as well: the telephone-survey process used by the company's market-research vendor was woefully inadequate. First, there was no way to close the loop with customers who identified themselves as detractors—no way to apologize, no way to develop a solution for whatever was troubling them. Second, the open-ended responses the vendor reported were intriguing, but managers had a tendency to read into them whatever they already believed. Third, the responses were often confusing and contradictory. For example, promoters frequently praised a product's simplicity, while detractors of that same product griped about its complexity. The teams obviously needed a way of drilling deeper if they were to understand the root causes of promotion and detraction.

In addition to these formal audits, some of the business units began to add the "would recommend" question to the brief transaction surveys they were already using to manage the quality of their interactions with customers. These responses provided a steady flow of NPS insights that illuminated hot spots and trouble spots relating to customers' experience with the company. For example, Intuit had decided to charge all QuickBooks customers for tech-support phone calls—even new customers who were having trouble getting the program up and running. Net Promoter Scores for customers who called tech support were drastically below the QuickBooks average, and it was immediately apparent that the policy was at fault. The business team tested several alternatives to see what effect they would have on scores; eventually the team found that the most economical solution was to offer free tech support for the first thirty days of ownership. Net Promoter Scores from customers who called tech support increased by more than thirty points as a result.

The Consumer Tax Group, home of the industry-leading Turbo-Tax product line, faced a particularly tough challenge. TurboTax's market share in the increasingly important Web-based segment had plummeted by more than 30 points from 2001 to 2003. Managers in the division knew that they had to get a better handle on customer issues. One successful initiative was the creation of a six-thousand-member "Inner Circle" of customers whose feedback would directly influence management decisions. Customers who registered to join this e-mail community were asked some basic demographics and were also asked the "would recommend" question so that the company could determine whether they were promoters, passives, or detractors. Then they were asked to suggest their highest-priority improvements for TurboTax and to vote on suggestions made by other Inner Circle members. Software sifted the suggestions and tracked the rankings, so that over time the most valuable ideas rose to the top of the list.

The results were eye-opening. For detractors, the top priority was improved quality of technical support. To address that issue, the management team reversed a decision made two years earlier and returned all phone tech-support functions from India to the United States and Canada. The team also boosted tech-support staffing levels. The second-biggest priority for detractors was to improve the installation process. That became a top priority for TurboTax's software engineers, who in the 2004 edition of the program achieved a reduction of nearly 50 percent in installation-related tech-support contacts.

Promoters had a different set of priorities. Topping the list was the rebate process: some complained that it took longer to fill out all the rebate forms than to install TurboTax and prepare their taxes! After getting this feedback, the division general manager assigned one person to own the rebate process and held that individual accountable for results. Soon the proof of purchase was simplified, the forms were redesigned, the whole process was streamlined—and turnaround time was reduced by several weeks.

The Consumer Tax Group continued to study Net Promoter Scores, examining various customer segments. New customers, the group found, had the lowest scores of any cluster. Executives called a sample of these customers to find out why, and what they discovered was startling and unsettling. All the features that had been added year after year to appeal to diverse customer groups with complex tax needs had yielded a product that no longer simplified the lives of standard filers. In fact, more than 30 percent of new customers never used the product a second time.

In response, the management team issued new priorities for the design engineers: make the program simpler. Soon the interview screens were revised according to new design principles. Confusing tax jargon was eliminated—a new editor hired from *People* magazine got the job of making the language clear and easy to understand. In tax year 2004, for the first time, the NPS of first-time users was even higher than that of longtime users. In addition, the company introduced a streamlined forms-based option for people with simple, straightforward tax returns. This new product, SnapTax, was released in tax year 2004 and generated an NPS of 64 percent—scoring higher with first-time users than TurboTax.

INTUIT'S RESULTS: HAPPY CUSTOMERS AND SHAREHOLDERS

Over the two-year period from the spring of 2003 to the spring of 2005, Net Promoter Scores for TurboTax jumped. The desktop version, for instance, rose from 46 to 61 percent. New users' scores climbed from 48 to 58 percent. Retail market share, which had been flat for years, surged from 70 to 79 percent—no easy feat in a maturing market. Scores improved at most of Intuit's major lines of business. Thanks to this success, Net Promoter Scores became part of the company's everyday operations. "Net Promoter gave us a tool to really focus organizational energy around building a better customer experience," said CEO Steve Bennett. "It provided actionable insights. Every business line [now] addresses this as part of their strategic plan; it's a component of every operating budget; it's part of every executive's bonus. We talk about progress on Net Promoter at every monthly operating review."

At the firm's 2004 Investor Day, when executives update securities analysts and major investors on the company's progress, challenges, and outlook for the future, Cook and Bennett unveiled their renewed commitment to building customer loyalty. They described how Net Promoter Scores had enabled the team to convert the historically soft goal of building better customer relationships into a hard, quantifiable process. Just as Six Sigma had helped Intuit improve its business processes to lower costs and enhance quality, Net Promoter Scores were helping it set priorities and measure progress toward the fundamental goal of stronger customer loyalty.

Yes, there was still a long way to go. But Cook and Bennett pointed out that the new initiative was simply a return to the original roots of Intuit's success. As the company grew larger, the need increased for a common metric that could help everyone balance today's profits against the improved customer relationships that feed future growth. "We have every customer metric under the sun," said Cook, "and yet we couldn't make those numbers focus the organization on our core value of doing right by the customer. The more metrics you track, the less relevant each one becomes. Each manager will choose to focus on the number that makes his decision look good. The concept of one single metric has produced a huge benefit for us—customers, employees, and investors alike."

By showcasing Net Promoter Scores as the central metric for revitalizing growth in the core businesses, Cook and Bennett were signaling to their own organization that this was not some here-today, gone-tomorrow corporate initiative. On the contrary: it was a business-critical priority so important to Intuit's future that it deserved to be understood by shareholders. Intuit's leaders were also signaling to shareholders that at the next Investor Day, these investors would be entitled to learn more about the company's progress on Net Promoter Scores.

Maybe the event even foreshadowed the day when all investors will insist on seeing reliable performance measures for customer-relationship quality—because only then can investors understand the economic prospects for profitable growth.

THREE

How the Net Promoter Score (NPS) Can Drive Growth

"**T**his is the best customer-relationship metric I've seen. I can't understand why any of you wouldn't want to try it!" The speaker was Jeff Immelt, chairman and CEO of General Electric. Immelt was leading the company's 2005 management conference in Boca Raton, Florida, and had just seen GE Healthcare's presentation on Net Promoter Scores.

Joe Hogan, the CEO of the $14 billion division, had been searching for a metric that would help focus his organization on building better relationships with its customers. For Hogan, "customers" meant the clinics and hospitals that purchased GE scanners and other diagnostic equipment. But many different individuals influenced these multimillion-dollar purchase decisions at each location—doctors and nurses, technical operators, the finance staff, and senior executives. The relationships Hogan wanted to build had to extend to all these people. How to gauge whether he was succeeding? Reading about the Net Promoter framework, Hogan thought it was a promising solution to this challenge. So he asked several executives in his organization to experiment with it. After six months of testing, he was sufficiently impressed with the results that he decided to roll it out around the world. He also made NPS a major component in the bonus formula for each of his direct reports.

In 2005, GE's initiative was still new. The jury is still out on what effects NPS will have over time. But it's likely to be a powerful tonic. For one thing, GE knows how to spread new metrics throughout the organization. It has begun rolling the initiative out across its divisions, and it will be asking its rising executives to study NPS in depth at its famous Crotonville leadership-training facility in New York. GE managers themselves are fully aware of the transformational power of metrics that connect to the core economics of a business. The company's renowned Six Sigma initiative, for instance, has led to dramatic increases in efficiency and quality. So when Hogan asked his chief quality officer to present his division's findings about NPS to GE's top 650 executives at the annual Boca meeting, he expected a response, and not just from Immelt. Sure enough: before long his phone was ringing off the hook as other divisions wanted to learn how they could adopt similar plans.

But there's another reason that GE is likely to pursue serious results from NPS. Ever since he succeeded Jack Welch as chief of the storied company, Immelt has been pushing for a cultural revolution. His goal is to revitalize the growth in GE's core businesses, thereby raising its organic growth rate from 5 to 8 percent a year. (*Organic growth* refers to growth in revenues from existing operations rather than from acquisitions.) In a company as large as GE, this goal will require not only a high level of innovation but the kind of relationships with customers that drive growth. Net Promoter Scores—a kind of Six Sigma for customer relationships—allow a company to measure and manage the process of building precisely the kind of relationships that are needed.

Gary Reiner, GE's corporate chief information officer and Six Sigma leader, is one of the executives Immelt has tapped to guide the success of customer metrics. Reiner explains his own assessment of NPS:

> *In a company of our size and complexity, it becomes critically important to simplify and focus on one number that is practical to measure. It is also vital that this metric reliably link to profits and growth. Our experience with satisfaction surveys has not been very good because they don't connect to business economics. But as we saw at GE Healthcare, NPS links well to both market share and profitability.*

This linkage, of course, is precisely what distinguishes Net Promoter Scores from conventional measures of customer satisfaction. Not only is NPS a simpler, more easily understood, and more actionable measure than customer-satisfaction ratings, but it also links directly to the economics of growth.

NPS AND GROWTH: THE EVIDENCE

When we began our research, our analysis of Net Promoter Scores focused only on how well customer-survey responses predicted actual referrals and repurchases. But the real test of NPS would be how well it explained relative growth rates for all competitors in an industry—and across a broader range of industry sectors than we had yet studied.

So we embarked on a new phase of the investigation. In the first quarter of 2001, our partner Satmetrix began tracking the "would recommend" scores of a new universe of customers— many thousands of them, representing four-hundred-plus companies in more than two dozen industries. Satmetrix had purchased e-mail addresses from public-list vendors and had recruited respondents by offering them a chance to win a $500 gift certificate at Amazon.com. In each subsequent quarter, its researchers gathered 10,000 to 15,000 responses to a very brief e-mail survey asking respondents to rate one or two companies with which they were familiar. (These names, too, were drawn from public sources.) By the end of 2003, they had built a database of more than 150,000 responses. Bain teams broke this database down into business sectors composed of direct competitors. We calculated Net Promoter Scores for every company that garnered at least 100 responses, then plotted each company's NPS against its revenue growth rate.

The results were striking. In airlines, for example, we found a very strong correlation between Net Promoter Scores and a company's average growth rate over the three-year period from 1999 to 2002 (see appendix A). Remarkably, this one simple statistic seemed to explain companies' relative growth rates across the entire industry; in other words, *no* airline had superior growth without a superior ratio of promoters to detractors. Not surprisingly, Southwest was the leader for this period. JetBlue wasn't included in the analysis, because it didn't exist at the beginning of the period, but a quick glimpse at recent performance reveals an NPS of 81 percent for JetBlue and a growth rate even higher than Southwest's.

We found much the same results in most of the industries we examined, including life insurance, personal computers, and Internet service providers. Dell, for example, has the highest NPS in its industry segment and by far the best growth.[1] The pattern is similar in many markets outside the United States. In 2004, a Bain team in London found that the ASDA chain (now owned by Wal-Mart Stores, Inc.) earned the highest NPS and had recorded the fastest growth among U.K. supermarket chains. In Korea, Samsung led the auto insurance business in both NPS and growth.

Finally, another Bain team examined all the industries for which the relationship between NPS and growth had been quantified. The team found that, on average, a twelve-point increase in NPS leads to a doubling in a company's rate of growth. Of course, averages can be deceiving, and competitors may not stand still. But this suggests the magnitude of the change that NPS improvement can help bring. At General Electric, Immelt wants to improve organic growth by three percentage points, from 5 to 8 percent, which amounts to a 60 percent increase in the company's organic-growth rate. So far, the GE divisions that have measured NPS range from the low single digits on up to 60 percent. If the company can generate ten points or more of NPS improvement across the board, it has a reasonable shot of reaching Immelt's growth target.

Let's be clear: NPS does not explain relative growth in every industry situation. Factors other than customer loyalty can play a role. Companies with monopolies and companies that dominate distribution channels, for instance, sometimes grow despite weak Net Promoter Scores. (Think of your local cable company.) And technological breakthroughs can create growth surges. But even in situations like these, it makes sense for companies to segment customers into promoters, passives, and detractors. Doing so will help managers generate faster and more efficient growth. No company can sustain its growth over a longer time frame and over multiple product-design and technology cycles without building good relationships. This explains why even the mighty Microsoft has decided to link executive compensation to customer-feedback scores. While loyalty isn't the only factor determining growth, profitable growth cannot long be maintained without it.

Another important caveat: a high NPS in and of itself is not the real objective, because a high NPS by itself is not the engine of growth. NPS merely measures the quality of a company's relationships with its customers. High-quality relationships are a necessary but not a sufficient condition for growth. A company may build such relationships, but it will squander the potential they create if it can't then make effective decisions, innovate, and do everything else necessary for growth.

THE ECONOMIC POWER OF HIGH-QUALITY RELATIONSHIPS

To understand the connection between customer relationships and growth, begin with a simple fact: in business, every decision ultimately involves economic trade-offs. Every company would want better relationships with customers if these relationships were free. Every CEO would prefer to meet earnings goals with good profits than with bad if there were no cost involved. Indeed, the abuse of customers would end tomorrow if ending it had no effect on companies' financial performance. But of course building high-quality relationships does cost something—often a considerable amount. It requires investment. It requires reducing a company's reliance on bad profits. There is no way to deceive or exploit customers and build better relationships with them at the same time.

But the real question is not just the costs but the benefits, and how the one stacks up against the other. Companies need to understand the economic value that results from building better customer relationships. They must be able to answer questions such as these: What would it be worth to raise our NPS by ten points? Where would this improvement show up in our financials? At the moment, few managers can answer these questions. This chapter will begin to clarify the economics in terms that numbers-oriented executives will understand.

First, however, it may help to see some real-life examples of how great customer relationships generate economic benefits.

The home-mortgage business provides one good illustration of the connection between good relationships and good economics. An average mortgage originator (salesperson) earns about $50,000 per year, with repeat customers and referrals accounting for between 20 and 40 percent of revenues. By contrast, the most successful mortgage originators can earn $1 million a year or more and typically generate at least 80 percent of their revenues from repeat customers or referrals. Getting customers to return—and getting them to bring their friends with them—completely changes the economics of the business for individual sales reps.

That kind of relationship building can also transform the economics of a company. Consider HomeBanc Mortgage Corporation, an Atlanta-based firm that traces its ancestry to a bank chartered in 1929. In the early 1990s HomeBanc was a small company with about 150 employees, only one office outside Georgia, and mortgage volume of about $500 million. By early 2005 the company had grown to some 1,200 employees, twenty-two branches in Georgia, Florida, and North Carolina, and more than $6 billion in mortgage volume. CEO Pat Flood's loyalty-based strategy depends heavily on repeat business and referrals, and it works. The company does little consumer advertising, yet growth in mortgage originations has exceeded 25 percent a year for the past decade, more than double the market average. The average NPS in the mortgage industry is 3 percent; HomeBanc's latest figure exceeds 80 percent.

The economic advantage of this kind of growth enables HomeBanc to invest a significant amount of time and money in training. As part of the company's boot-camp-style training programs, for instance, new recruits spend seven to nine weeks at corporate headquarters before making solo calls on their first customer. The training—coupled with careful hiring—leads to high-caliber service, infrequent errors, and happy customers. Repeat business and referrals, in turn, allow HomeBanc to record productivity levels 60 percent higher than recent industry standards. As a result, compensation of mortgage originators is well above industry norms.

HomeBanc has effectively eliminated bad profits by offering a money-back guarantee. Any customer can reclaim the $375 application fee if he or she is dissatisfied for any reason. Fewer than 0.5 percent of HomeBanc's customers claim this refund. The company piles up good profits with loan-loss rates more than 20 percent below industry averages. Already a market leader in Georgia, it is rapidly expanding in both Florida and North Carolina.

High-quality customer relationships can transform the economics of retailing as well. Costco, the wholesale-club company, boasts an NPS of 79 percent and has grown to 45 million members despite spending little on advertising or marketing. While a typical big-box supermarket carries forty thousand SKUs, Costco stores have only forty-five hundred—only those items on which it can provide outstanding value. Sales per store are almost twice those at Wal-Mart's Sam's Club, its closest competitor. Costco's success funds a generous compensation package for its employees. New hires start at $10 an hour—high for the retail industry—and progress to $40,000 a year after three years. They receive a benefits package virtually unequalled in the industry. Low turnover and long tenure reduce hiring and training costs and boost productivity; they also contribute to Costco's remarkably low inventory-shrinkage rate, which is only 13 percent of the industry average. The company eliminates bad profits through a generous return policy—there is no time limit on returns except for a limit of six months on computer technology items. Costco's earnings grew at 16.5 percent a year from 1994 to 2004, while the stock-price gains exceeded 20 percent a year.

The storyline is much the same at every company that has built communities of good relationships. Enterprise Rent-A-Car charges less than competitors, pays its employees far more, and has grown so fast that it is now the largest single buyer of cars and light trucks in the United States. Chick-fil-A was able to grow nearly 15 percent annually between 1994 and 2004, despite ranking near the bottom of its industry in national marketing expenditures as a percentage of sales. The company generates superior profits in the price-sensitive fast-food business while helping the average operator of a freestanding restaurant earn more than $170,000 a year, far more than comparable managers at competitors. Both companies have recorded Net Promoter Scores well above the rest of the industry. Clearly, superior relationships drive economic advantage in ways that leave the competition mystified.

WHY NPS WORKS

Let's strip away the mystery. The value of a promoter or a detractor can be quantified. Given the vital role of word of mouth, indeed, NPS *must* be quantified. You may not have all the data you need at your fingertips, but most companies are able to produce it. If exact figures aren't available, use reasonable estimates.

The first step is to calculate the lifetime value of your average customer. This process is described in chapter 2 of my book *The Loyalty Effect* and in many other books as well. The fundamental approach is to tally up all the cash flows that occur over the life of a typical customer relationship, then to convert this total into today's dollars using a reasonable discount rate.

The next step is to understand that the lifetime value of an average customer by itself isn't very useful. In fact, promoters and detractors exhibit dramatically different behaviors and produce dramatically different economic results. The following list describes several factors that distinguish promoters and detractors and offers some tips for estimating their economic effects on your business.

- *Retention rate.* Detractors generally defect at higher rates than promoters, which means that they have shorter and less profitable relationships with a company. By tagging customers as promoters or detractors on the basis of their response to the "would recommend" question, you can determine true retention patterns over time and quantify their impact. You can estimate the average tenure of your current population of detractors and promoters even before gathering the time-series data. Just ask them on the same survey with the "would recommend" question how long they've been customers, and then use this average tenure to infer likely retention patterns.

- *Margins.* Promoters are usually less price-sensitive than other customers because they believe they are getting good value overall from the company. The opposite is true for detractors: they're more price-sensitive. You'll need to examine the market basket of goods or services purchased by promoters and detractors over a six- to twelve-month period and then calculate the margin on each basket, keeping track of discounts and price concessions.

- *Annual spend.* Promoters increase their purchases more rapidly than detractors. The reason is that they tend to consolidate more of their category purchases with their favorite supplier. Your share of wallet increases as promoters upgrade to higher-priced products and respond to cross-selling efforts. Promoters' interest in new product offerings and brand extensions far exceeds that of detractors or passives.

- *Cost efficiencies.* Detractors complain more frequently, thereby consuming customer-service resources. Some companies also find that credit losses are higher for detractors. (Perhaps that is how the detractors exact revenge.) Customer-acquisition costs are also lower for promoters, due to both the longer duration of their relationships and their role in generating referrals.

- *Word of mouth.* This component of NPS merits a somewhat more detailed consideration because it is so important and because it seems to be the one that stumps most analysts. Begin by quantifying (by survey if necessary) the proportion of new customers who selected your firm because of reputation or referral. The lifetime value of these new customers, including any savings in sales or marketing expense, should be allocated to promoters. (Between 80 and 90 percent of positive referrals come from promoters.) Keep in mind that referred customers usually have superior economics themselves; they also have a higher propensity to become promoters, which accelerates the positive spiral of referrals.

  Detractors, meanwhile, are responsible for 80 to 90 percent of the negative word of mouth, and the cost of this drag on growth should be allocated to them. Perhaps the easiest way to estimate the cost is to determine how many positive comments are neutralized by one negative comment and how many potential referrals have therefore been lost. This number can be accurately determined only through customer interviews, but for an initial estimate it's safe to assume that each negative comment neutralizes from three to ten positives. For example, consider the process you might go through in searching for a dentist when you move to a new town. If you hear one negative comment about a particular dentist from a trusted friend or colleague, how many positive comments will you need to hear before you select that dentist?

WORD-OF-MOUTH ECONOMICS AT DELL

Though all this calculation may sound complex, it doesn't need to be. To show how it is done, a Bain team used the approach to quantify the value of promoters and detractors in the personal-computer business. The team used only publicly available data so that what it did could serve as a model for companies that lack sophisticated databases. Indeed, the same approach can be used by prospective investors—even by competitors—to understand a firm's customer-relationship economics.

The Bain team focused on the industry leader, Dell, and calculated the value of detractors and promoters for Dell's consumer business utilizing the economic model displayed in exhibit 3-1. While securities analysts estimate that the average consumer is worth $210 to Dell, in fact a detractor costs the company $57 while a promoter generates $328. Let's review the process the Bain team followed, focusing especially on the economics of word of mouth. This word-of-mouth factor was the biggest source of difference between the average value of a customer (based on conventional accounting methods) and the true economic value of promoters and detractors.

The team first worked with Satmetrix to develop a brief e-mail survey that screened public lists for Dell customers. Researchers then asked those customers a series of questions, including why

EXHIBIT 3-1

NPS economics

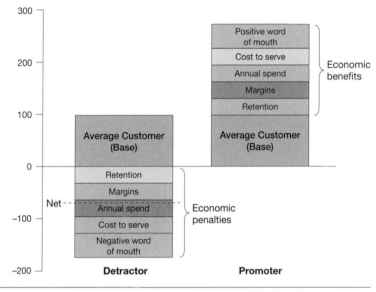

they had selected Dell over its competitors. The results showed that a little more than 25 percent of Dell's new customers came to the company through referral from friends or colleagues. The survey also asked the "would recommend" question to determine the customer's status as promoter, passive, or detractor, along with how many positive or negative comments they had made to friends or colleagues. The responses revealed that 60 percent of Dell's customers were promoters, 25 percent were passives, and 15 percent were detractors.[2] Based on the number of positive and negative comments reported by these promoters, passives, and detractors, the team then estimated that the 8 million consumers who were Dell customers at the beginning of 2003 made about 40 million positive and 5 million negative comments.

Now, here's a step-by-step calculation of the value of this positive word of mouth:

- In our survey, 25 percent of new customers said the primary reason they chose Dell was referral. So 1 million of the 4 million new customers Dell acquired in 2003 came from positive word of mouth.

- Since each new customer is worth an average of $210 each, those 1 million new customers were worth $210 million to the company.

- If 40 million positive comments generated $210 million in value, each positive comment was worth $5.25.

- Given that the average promoter reported making positive comments to about eight people a year, the promoter's positive word of mouth is worth $42 ($8 \times \$5.25$).

The survey also asked customers about their average annual spending, their tenure, and the number of times they called Dell's customer support, all of which enabled the team to estimate the other economic advantages shown in exhibit 3-1. Overall, the researchers found that promoters were worth $118 more than an average customer, or $328. If this analysis were done with Dell's internal data, the number would probably be higher, since it would be possible to quantify the superior value of referred customers over time. It would also be possible to track more accurately the repeat-purchase behaviors of promoters.

When estimating the cost of detractors, the researchers first found that detractors accounted for most of Dell's negative word of mouth. To estimate the cost of these negative comments, the survey asked customers how many positive comments from friends or colleagues were required to neutralize each negative comment. On average, customers reported that it required at least five positive comments to neutralize one negative. Since survey data indicated that each detractor made negative comments to about four people a year, each detractor was neutralizing twenty positive comments that would have been worth $5.25 each. So on this count alone, each detractor was costing the company $105 a year.

The survey also revealed that detractors called customer-service reps almost three times more frequently than average customers, spent less per year, and were less likely to repurchase from Dell. Over the life of their relationship with Dell, detractors generated a total of $267 less than average customers, meaning that each detractor actually was destroying $57 in value for Dell and its shareholders.

This calculation surely underestimates the full cost of detractors. Our analysis ignored the effect of negative word of mouth on existing customers; it ignored the negative spillover that unhappy consumers might have on Dell's corporate business; and it ignored any negative impact of dealing with unhappy customers on the motivation and commitment of Dell employees. Nevertheless, it provides a reasonable estimate for evaluating investments targeted to building better relationships.

The Bain team's approach reveals the powerful economics of customer promoters. In 2003, as noted, Dell had about 8 million individual customers. The 15 percent who were detractors cost the company about $68 million (1.2 million detractors at $57 loss per detractor). Converting just half of those detractors into average customers—not an unrealistic target, given that other companies with high Net Promoter Scores typically generate only 3 to 8 percent detractors—would add more than $160 million annually to the bottom line (600,000 detractors at $267 improvement per conversion). This simple math could help Dell managers place the right level of priority on reducing detractors and increasing promoters. Dell or any other company can evaluate major investments aimed at improving the customer experience, because these proposals can now be subjected to the same rigorous economic analysis already applied to other investments.

In short, by moving beyond traditional customer-satisfaction surveys and by rigorously tracking NPS, you can finally create a link between customer feedback and cash flow. You can begin to squeeze bad profits out of your income statement and tune up your growth engine for consistently superior performance.

NPS AND MARKET SHARE

The goal of most corporate strategies is to build competitive advantage and to gain the highest market share possible. The irony is this: the more successful a company's strategy, the more likely the company will stumble into the trap of bad profits. Even if CEOs have no desire to book bad profits, because they recognize the deleterious effects bad profits have on growth, they and their executive team are always under pressure to grow earnings. That alone makes executives susceptible to the temptation to milk customer relationships.

At the extreme, great strategies often create monopolies or near monopolies. If you want to fly nonstop from Boston to Phoenix, you have only one choice of airline. If you want to replace the battery on your Apple iPod, you don't have many options. You may find that only one mobile-phone provider offers you good reception at your home, at your office, and during your commute. If that provider insists on a two-year contract in return for a reasonable pricing plan, it has essentially trapped you in a temporary monopoly. All such strategies generate substantial profits, but the customers who pay for them are more vulnerable than ever to abusive, manipulative, and coercive treatment. The cell-phone provider with the best network coverage, for example, is more likely to offer lackadaisical service, complicated billing, onerous overage and roaming fees, and unhelpful customer-service reps.

Does it make sense for such companies, which have earned or bought their way to dominance in particular markets, to invest in building good relationships? Or are they better off simply maximizing near-term profits? Consider the cable TV companies that negotiated exclusive contracts with municipal governments. In cable, there is little historical correlation between relative growth and relative Net Promoter Scores because growth is driven more by increases in population and income in a given market than by the cable company's service levels. Indeed, Net Promoter Scores in the cable industry are embarrassingly low, averaging negative 6 percent. Customers are rarely enthusiastic when they have limited choice—and anyway, many local cable companies have ratcheted up prices while providing mediocre service.

But no monopoly lasts forever. New technologies emerge. Regulations change. Building good customer relationships prepares a company for the possibility of increased competition. What's more, superior NPS boosts a company's growth potential by enabling it to expand into adjacent service areas. For example, one of the most profitable expansion opportunities for cable companies has been to move into the telecommunications business— and it turns out that NPS works well to explain companies' relative success in this market. Bain teams analyzed a series of local telephone markets in the United States and Canada, examining the rate at which the local cable firm was able to cross-sell telecom services to existing customers. The best single explanation of relative success was the difference between the NPS the cable company received from its core cable customers and the NPS given the local phone company by its core phone customers. We call this difference the *Net Promoter delta*. Where the delta was positive—with the cable NPS higher than the phone company's NPS—the cable company's telecom penetration was rapid. The bigger the delta, the faster the penetration.[3]

NPS leaders recognize the value of market-share leadership. Intuit enjoys 70 percent retail market share or more in its top three businesses, and Southwest Airlines has an 80 percent share of take-offs and landings at its top twenty-five airports. Enterprise has overwhelming leadership in the home-market sector of car rentals. But what keeps these firms growing is not their worship of market share; it is their ability to keep their people focused on earning good profits. Good customer relationships not only expand the core business; they open the door for successful extensions into adjacent businesses. (Another example is Enterprise's profitable expansion into airport rentals and used-car sales.) Superior market share is an excellent goal. To achieve it, and to sustain it, you must find a way to track NPS and build better relationships—not only because it is the right thing to do, but because it makes economic sense.

HOW TO MEASURE

RESPONSES

FOUR

The Enterprise Story—
Measuring What Matters

Turnberry Isle Resort, Florida, 1996. The mood at the Enterprise Rent-A-Car senior management retreat should have been festive. It was Enterprise's most successful year so far. The company was growing fast and had just overtaken Hertz as the number one rental-car agency in the United States. But the opening presentation at the meeting hit a sobering note. Customer-satisfaction scores were flatlining. In a satisfaction study of insurance adjusters (a prime source of customer referrals), some adjusters had ranked Enterprise below one of its competitors.

When that slide hit the screen, CEO Andy Taylor remembers, "there was an audible gasp in the room." All eyes turned toward founder and chairman Jack Taylor, Andy's father, who had devoted his life to building a company that would serve customers better than any other. Jack was upset. After the morning presentations, Jack met privately with Andy, and his message was short. "Andrew," he said, ever the paterfamilias, "we've got a *big* problem."[1]

Andy Taylor, who hadn't been called Andrew by his father (or anyone else) since childhood, remembers this as a defining moment. He had been named president and chief operating officer of the closely held company in 1980, CEO in 1991. Now, he knew, it was up to him to change things. He vowed to ensure that Enterprise set new standards of excellence in service and customer relationships. The only question was how to go about it.

The company had been experimenting with customer-satisfaction surveys ever since 1989, when it first began marketing car rentals to consumers. But back then, many managers doubted that the surveys really meant much. Sure, the numbers indicated a few problems. But wasn't the company growing? Wasn't it making money? Any difficulties, some of the managers said, weren't systemic; they could be addressed locally. That was more in keeping with Enterprise's decentralized tradition.

But by the early 1990s Andy Taylor was worried, partly because he himself had been hearing more complaints than usual from customers. So he assigned a team of senior managers to work on the surveys. That team designed a new instrument—and like a lot of such instruments, it suffered from "question creep." The initial version, one page long, included nine questions and asked for seventeen separate responses, including an open-ended "How could we have served you better?" At the top, however, was the question that would turn out to be central to the whole endeavor: "Overall, how satisfied were you with your recent car rental from Enterprise?" The five boxes a customer could check ran from "completely satisfied" to "completely dissatisfied." Taylor and his team decided that the company would calculate the percentages in each category for this question. They would call the scores the Enterprise Service Quality index, or ESQi.

Thus did Enterprise launch the measurement process, as Taylor later told *Fortune Small Business,* that "enabled us to go from being a nearly $2 billion business in 1994 to a $7 billion-plus business" in 2004.[2] But in 1994, there was still a long ways to go. Making ESQi into a useful, credible tool turned out to be a long, involved, and contentious process.

LEARNING TO MEASURE

Enterprise's first questionnaires went out in July 1994, and the company reported its first three months' worth of results to senior managers in October. Overall, the ratings were only fair. 86 percent of respondents were at least moderately satisfied. But only 60 percent checked the "top box," as the company called it, to indicate they were completely satisfied. That score, Taylor felt, was far lower than it should be.

Worse, there were huge disparities between the various regions, with some registering top-box scores in the 80 percents and others in the low 50s. One of the company's biggest and most profitable regions came in at a dismal 54 percent. "We were pretty much at or near the bottom of the whole company," acknowledged the region's senior vice president for rental. "To competitive people like us, that was a real difficult pill to swallow, especially in front of our peers."

Maybe not surprisingly, the first reaction among some managers was to shoot the messenger. Low scorers, Taylor remembers, "ripped the measurement, the survey questionnaire, and the sampling technique behind it." The process didn't allow for differences in branch size, the managers argued. It didn't take into account that different regions of the country might have different expectations about customer service. Besides, they added, what did it all prove? ESQi might be a valid measurement of satisfaction, but did it have anything to do with growing the company? Was there really a connection between customer satisfaction and financial results?

So Taylor and his team continued to examine and refine their methods. They found that branch size and geographical region didn't matter—top performers and poorer ones could be found in any category. The team challenged the notion that senior managers already knew where the problems lay. When asked to rank their various operations above or below the company's service average without looking at the latest ESQi scores, for example, the managers couldn't peg more than half, the same as guessing.

The team also made three changes that would prove definitively important:

- Since the customer experience was primarily controlled by the local branch, team members reasoned, the company needed to score not just its regions but each of its several thousand branches. (Enterprise at the time had more than eighteen-hundred branches; today it has well over six thousand.) Only with this degree of granularity could regional managers reliably hold the branches accountable for building good customer relationships. Each branch, moreover, would need feedback from at least twenty-five customers a month, so the sample size had to increase. A three-month moving average of this feedback would produce a reliable ranking.

- Listening to their field managers, the team also decided that the information had to be more timely. Customer-satisfaction scores that were gathered once a quarter and disseminated long after the quarter's end didn't really tell you much. Who could remember what had happened during that quarter to move the scores one way or the other? In fact, Taylor and his team wanted data in as close to real time as possible, so that frontline staffers could remember events that had influenced the feedback. Timely feedback would also allow branches to test new ideas and then to evaluate them when the survey scores arrived. To speed things up, the researchers switched from mail to telephone surveys and began reporting ESQi monthly, just like the monthly reporting of profits and other performance measures.

- Finally, since executives wanted proof that investments to increase ESQi scores would actually pay off, the team analyzed how well various questions on the surveys linked to customer behaviors such as repurchases and referrals—behaviors that drove growth. Researchers called back hundreds of customers who had taken the survey months earlier, asking how many positive and negative referrals those customers had made. They asked the customers how many cars they had rented since taking the survey and what Enterprise's share of those rentals had been. These questions struck pay dirt: the one question at the top of the page, "Were you completely satisfied?" accounted for a startling 86 percent of the variation in customer referrals and repurchases. Those who gave the company a perfect 5 on a 5-point scale—the equivalent of promoters—were three times more likely to return to Enterprise than a customer giving a lower score. And nearly 90 percent of positive referrals were made by top-box customers. The bottom line: high top-box scores translated directly into growth and profit.

All these findings quieted the skeptical executives. The measurements meant something. But nothing actually seemed to be *improving* the company's scores, as the 1996 meeting showed. So Andy Taylor's next challenge was to get his executives and his branches to do something about the measurements. It was, he wrote, a "time for leadership, time to put some teeth into our efforts."

TAKING ESQI SERIOUSLY

Taylor's first step was to link ESQi scores to corporate recognition. At Enterprise, the granddaddy of recognition programs is the prestigious President's Award, a coveted prize given to people who make truly exceptional contributions to the company. After 1996, you weren't eligible unless your branch or region was at or above the corporate average for ESQi. Southern California's Group 32, which had won a disproportionate number of these awards in the past, came up empty-handed for the following two years. The point hit home. "People said, 'You know what? This company is serious about ESQi,'" remembered Tim Walsh, a former officer of Group 32.

Step two delivered an even stronger message. The company redesigned its monthly operating reports to highlight ESQi, listing every branch's score right alongside the net profit numbers. The reports ranked every branch, region, and group manager in the company, so everyone immediately knew how he or she stacked up against everyone else. Moreover, the company announced that no one with a below-average ESQi score was eligible for promotion— and backed up its announcement by passing over a well-regarded California executive who Taylor says "would have been a shoo-in under the old system."

Step three: communication and more communication. "ESQi became a key topic of *every* speech I gave internally," says Taylor. "Customer satisfaction went on the agenda of *every* management and operations review meeting at all levels. When I was present, I would go right to the bottom of the ESQi rankings and pointedly ask the managers responsible to explain what was going on and what they were doing about it. Those were apt to be the first questions in a sustained grilling."

Before long, ESQi was an inextricable part of Enterprise's corporate culture. The promotion requirement of above-average

ESQi came to be known as "jacks or better," as in the traditional poker-table requirement of a pair of jacks or better to open the betting. The branches or groups that were below average and thus ineligible for promotions were said to be in "ESQi jail." And gradually, ESQi scores began to improve. In 1994 the average had been around 67. By 1998 it had risen to 72, and by 2002 it hit 77. The gap between top performers and those at the bottom narrowed, shrinking from 28 points in 1994 to only 12 in 2001. Even Southern California brought its number up to above average, and again was winning some President's Awards.

WHY ESQI WORKS

Enterprise's ESQi system is designed to help frontline managers pursue two objectives: get more top-box ratings and fewer scores of neutral or worse. In the language of this book, the goals are to increase the number of customer promoters and reduce the number of detractors. The most effective example I have yet seen of a relationship-measurement process, ESQi has several distinctive features.

Tight focus. Unlike much market research, ESQi is not designed by headquarters staff to address every question or pet project someone in the company might have. Quite the opposite. Over time, the company dropped all those questions on the initial questionnaire in favor of just one: how satisfied were you with your most recent rental experience? If the customer is dissatisfied, the surveyor expresses regret and says, we would like to have someone give you a call about this whenever it would be convenient. That's it. If marketing or any other department wants to learn about other issues, Enterprise commissions separate customized research. In effect, the customer survey was transformed from a market-research instrument to a practical scoring tool—an operating system.

Operational accountability. The organizational process for managing the research was similarly transformed. Since it was line managers who would be relying on the tool, ESQi was moved out of the market-research department entirely. Dan Gass, the manager responsible for running the new system, reports directly to Jim Runnels, the operating executive responsible for Enterprise's rental business. While the phone surveys themselves are handled by an outside vendor, Gass stays closely involved. He regularly visits the vendor's facility to talk with the phone staff. He monitors calls at least fifteen hours a month. This alerts him to any major issues that require executive attention, and it helps him discover ways to improve the overall process.

Timeliness and high participation rates. Enterprise computers regularly upload a random sample of recently closed rental tickets to the survey vendor to ensure that customers are surveyed within a few days of renting a car. Because the survey is so short, the rate of customer cooperation exceeds 95 percent. The high response rate eliminates sample bias and enhances the reliability of scores.

The closed loop. One decision that was critical to ESQi's success was not to ask the survey vendor to diagnose the root causes of a customer's score. Much to the vendor's dismay, Taylor and his team insisted that attempting to generate both the score and the diagnosis with the same survey would lead to failure on both counts.

The reasoning was compelling. Anyone who has done root-cause analysis knows that it takes at least four or five follow-up questions to determine the problem that needs attention. And probing for the root cause of an individual customer's concerns often requires knowing something about both the customer and the transaction. For example, it may be essential to know whether the branch was temporarily understaffed, whether the transaction was a first-time rental, or what the customer's historic rental pattern has been. No outside phone interviewer can possibly have all that knowledge and understanding.

So whenever a customer communicates any dissatisfaction on the ESQi survey, the phone rep asks the "would you accept a call" question. More than 90 percent of these customers agree to be called—at which point an e-mail alert, including the customer's phone number and the survey score, is automatically forwarded to the branch involved. Branch managers have been trained to call right away, to apologize, to probe for the root cause of the customer's disappointment, and then to develop an appropriate solution. In some cases, the apology itself is all it takes to fix the problem. In others, a free rental is more appropriate. The primary diagnosis is always performed at the front line so that the branch can learn what needs to be fixed and fix it.

A link to the economics of the business. Thanks to the closed loop, Enterprise has been highly successful in reducing detractors: the proportion of customers who rate their experience neutral or worse has declined from 12 to 5 percent since 1994. This drop by itself has improved the firm's economics—there is less negative word of mouth. The increase in the percentage of promoters also improves the economics, both by driving growth and by reducing costs. For instance, Enterprise can spend less on advertising than Hertz and still grow faster due to Enterprise's word-of-mouth advantage. Measuring and managing the number of customer promoters created at each branch allows the company to turn word of mouth from a soft benefit into a quantifiable competitive weapon.

Continuous evolution. Of course, the system is constantly evolving and is much more effective today than it was when it started. Call efficiency has grown from twelve completed calls per hour in 1996 to almost twenty today, which means that the cost per branch to run the system is less than $550 per year. Enterprise has also continued its drive to deliver more timely data. A while ago, the corporate average seemed stuck at 77 percent. As Dan Gass searched for explanations for this stall, he noticed a seasonal effect: most branches' scores dropped off during the summer. Summer was a time when a lot of new hires were coming on board and attention was drifting away from ESQi. To maintain the focus on customer service, Gass pushed Enterprise to report ESQi at the regional level on a weekly basis. In 2004, with this new data available, there was no decline in summer scores. Simply generating the numbers more frequently to keep the organization focused did the trick. By November, the company was averaging nearly 80 percent top-box results.

HOW ESQI DRIVES IMPROVEMENT

ESQi itself, of course, is only a measurement; the real challenge is to keep on improving the scores. Enterprise's improvement efforts fall into several categories:

- *Training.* Gass developed a comprehensive training program around the concept of the service cycle. Enterprise employees interact with customers at a whole series of points during a rental, from the initial call on through pickup, arrival at the branch, signing the contract, and so on. The training program sets standards for each point in the cycle and includes tips on how employees can ensure a pleasant experience for the customer at every step.

- *On-the-spot fixes.* Managers discourage the use of customer-survey language in their branches. Branch employees won't just ask a customer if he or she was completely satisfied; they'll probe for what they can do to make the rental experience better, and then take immediate action. The goal is to make sure that customers come back repeatedly and tell their friends. But management also watches costs, because there is little benefit to any Enterprise manager who runs a branch that gets a high ESQi score but isn't also growing profitably.

- *Experimentation.* Individuals and teams try new approaches, new tactics, and new strategies, then watch to see whether these changes improve outcomes. In effect, Enterprise's more than six thousand branches and twelve monthly feedback scores allow more than seventy-two thousand experiments to drive learning every year. Experimentation is particularly important when it comes to generating more promoters. Detractors presumably want their problems solved, but what do promoters want? As it turns out, generating promoters requires initiatives such as offering a free bottle of chilled water on the shuttle bus. This idea was pioneered by a driver who experimented with putting a small cooler in his bus; his branch's growing ESQi score alerted others to the success of the innovation. In fact, most of Enterprise's enhanced services, including picking you up at your home, office, or repair shop, bubbled up from individual branch successes.

- *Closing the loop even faster.* If you rent from Enterprise, you'll experience an interesting phenomenon: when you drop off your car at the end of the rental, you will probably be asked two or three questions by the crew member who processes your return. How was our service? What could we have done to make your experience better? If there was a problem, how can we make it up to you? The crew member will make every effort to correct any complaints on the spot. In most branches, this kind of direct feedback is tabulated at the end of each day; it provides the agenda for the next morning's pre-opening team huddle.

- *Learning from the best.* Enterprise has found that the best ideas rarely come down from headquarters executives; they are developed, field-tested, and revised out in the branches. The trick for the company is to create forums in which the really good ideas can be identified and shared. This is why Enterprise spends so much time on ESQi at area, regional, and national manager meetings—and why the results are widely published. At national gatherings, some session leaders ask branch managers to display their ESQi scores on their name tags. Branch managers at these meetings thus know at a glance who has something to teach them. The ranking system ensures that when managers are looking for good ideas, they seek advice from the branches with the best scores rather than from those who are best at spinning impressive stories.

Since Enterprise links customer-feedback scores to promotions, it's surprising that you don't hear employees pleading with customers for top-box ratings. But unlike car dealers, Enterprise branches don't post sample surveys on the wall with the top boxes suggestively filled in. Instead, Enterprise teaches its employees that manipulating scores is not only unethical—as unethical as stealing from the cash register or fudging profits—but also contrary to the real goal of their company, which is to provide a superior customer experience.

Of course, some employees have been tempted to bend the rules and game their results. Enterprise calls this *speeding* and regards it as grounds for dismissal. Shortly after the branch-specific process was implemented, for example, it was rumored that a few branches were changing phone numbers on the records of unhappy customers. A number altered by only one digit meant that a phone surveyor would never connect and the branch would avoid a bad score. At Enterprise, though, it's difficult to hide this kind of malfeasance for long, since employees are frequently transferred across branches and anyone caught doctoring phone numbers can be fired. The company now keeps track of how many phone numbers fail to connect to the customer of record, identifies outlier branches, and scrutinizes their process.

As another safeguard against gaming, area managers occasionally ask to have the customer-exception reports forwarded to them for follow-up, and then talk directly to detractors. The executives also call a few customers randomly to ask about their experience. ESQi, like any system, is effective only if the input is pure and honest," says Andy Taylor. Indeed, any question about the appropriateness of gaming ESQi would appear to be covered by the company's value statement: "Personal honesty and integrity are the foundation of the company's success." To deter any attempt at loose interpretation, Taylor expects his top managers to continually reinforce the importance of the integrity of ESQi. Stories about attempts to game the system—and the career-ending consequences—become tribal knowledge at regional gatherings of branch managers. The stories are repeated so often that everyone understands the consequences of cheating on ESQi.

VOTE FOR GROWTH

One of the most significant breakthroughs in building effective teamwork at Enterprise branches is a recently developed process known as "The Vote."

Neil Leyland, a manager overseeing several branches in London, noticed a conundrum: his branch employees always seemed to think their ESQi scores should be higher than they were, but their scores never seemed to move much. Leyland decided that the employees weren't working together as effectively as they could be in each branch. Nor were they holding each other accountable for results.

So he came up with a plan. Every Monday morning, before his branches opened, each of the team members was asked to rank-order all the others, from best to worst, based on the quality of their customer service over the past week. The votes were tallied and posted for all to see. Leyland asked employees to keep their comments positive, to explain the rationale for their rankings, and to provide specific examples of good and bad behaviors. Typical comments included: "I rated you last because I noticed that you didn't answer the phone before the third ring several times, and I had to leave my customer to cover for you." Or "You seem to have a hard time looking the customer in the eye when you shake his hand." The group worked hard to ensure that their comments were constructive, and everyone had to offer suggestions to the team-mates whom they ranked below average. On subsequent Mondays, Leyland presented awards to the top-rated employee and to the employee whose rankings were most improved that week.

At first, other managers found this mutual feedback extreme. Some feared that the program would lead to contentious, uncon-structive behavior or would wreck team spirit. But soon Leyland's laggard branches rocketed from the bottom to the top of the ESQi rankings, and their annual growth rate accelerated to more than 50 percent. When Dan Gass saw those numbers, he became a believer—and so did many branch managers throughout the sys-tem. Some managers implemented The Vote but chose to gather the rankings confidentially and share only the final tallies. Most found that an open ballot was the most effective at making each team member feel personally accountable for creating change.

Within two years, more than half of Enterprise's worldwide branches had adopted The Vote as a core tool for improving customer service. Today, some of the same senior managers who feared that the process would be too extreme are inviting top-ranked employees out to lunch. That provides both a reward for the employees and a source of new ideas for the managers. For example, one winner routinely noted personal details on the customer's rental contract (like "visiting son in hospital") as a reminder to ask how the visit went when the car was returned.

Back in the United Kingdom, meanwhile, Enterprise continues its upward trajectory. With The Vote driving performance, Enterprise handily outstripped its competitors on an independent assessment of its NPS (exhibit 4-1). Growing at an average of 20 percent

EXHIBIT 4-1

The NPS of various U.K. car rentals

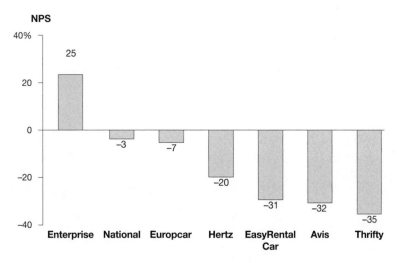

Source: Leading Edge survey, November 2004, commisioned by Bain & Company, Inc.

per year while the competition has been shrinking, Enterprise thus has consistently gained market share. Many companies have been unable to repeat their success in one country when they set up shop in another. Enterprise seems to have found the secret.

A UNIQUE SYSTEM

Enterprise's homegrown system of assessing customer relationships differs a little from the system I describe in this book. Enterprise doesn't use the terms *promoters* and *detractors*. It relies on a 5-point scale rather than the 0-to-10 scale used by Intuit and others. ESQi is based only on top-box results—the percentage of promoters— rather than *net* promoters, or promoters minus detractors. I believe that the extra step of calculating a Net Promoter Score is worth the trouble, because it ensures that a company will pay attention to both groups and because NPS correlates with growth rates more closely than does the number of promoters alone.

But no one can argue with success. Indeed, the more closely one studies Enterprise's ESQi measurement process, the more impressive it becomes. The company's closed-loop system ensures that measurements tie into action. Improvements keep bubbling up from the branches. The percentage of customers who are pro- moters continues to expand. And even though Enterprise doesn't include its detractors in the ESQi score, it pays close attention to them and works to cut their number by reducing operational mistakes.

Andy Taylor credits ESQi as the single biggest reason that Enterprise has been able to maintain superior growth in its core business despite its enormous scale. ESQi has enabled his branches to focus their creativity on delivering a better customer experi- ence, not on artificially boosting accounting profits. The resulting customer loyalty has allowed the firm to expand into adjacent markets, such as airport rentals and used-car sales, with the wind at its back. By jettisoning traditional satisfaction-survey methods and replacing them with one reliable number, Enterprise continues to grow, to prosper, and to set the industry standard for generating more promoters and fewer detractors.

FIVE

Why Satisfaction Surveys Fail

Enterprise Rent-A-Car's ESQi system has created a buzz in corporate boardrooms. Business leaders are asking whether they, too, should have a system to measure the quality of customer relationships. They are turning to their marketing or service-quality staff for the answer. Big mistake.

It's not the question that is flawed but the direction of inquiry. Remember that the marketing department was not responsible for the success story at Enterprise. On the contrary: ESQi was created only after the job was taken out of marketing and given to operating managers. Line managers need to trust the system if they are to make the changes necessary to improve scores. Line managers are the people who can best shift priorities and invest in upgrading the overall customer experience. To be sure, marketing must be involved in developing the right feedback system, as it was at Enterprise. But so must the leaders of process quality and finance, along with the line executives.

The temptation for too many staff vice presidents is to do what they did in the past—turn to satisfaction-survey vendors for their latest prepackaged solution. Trouble is, it's exactly this simplistic approach that has given us a business world rife with bad profits, Net Promoter Scores averaging less than 10 percent, and growth rates in the low single digits. Would companies be in the pickle they're in if satisfaction surveys really made a difference?

The purpose of this chapter is thus to hammer home the point that you cannot build an effective customer-feedback system on the shaky foundation of current satisfaction-survey methods and practices. In the best tradition of late-night comedy, here are the top ten reasons that satisfaction surveys are a joke.

#10: TOO MANY SURVEYS, TOO MANY QUESTIONS

A senior marketing executive at Chick-fil-A loves his new BMW, his third. What he doesn't love is the constant pestering from BMW surveyors who ask dozens of questions to determine just how satisfied he really is with the car. Like so many customers, he gets long phone calls, usually at dinner time, one after every service visit, even including a presurvey that coached him on how to answer the questions on subsequent surveys. At this point, he says, he would have been most satisfied if BMW had simply reduced the price of the car by the amount it spends on surveys. As a marketing exec, though, he was also sensitive to the subtext BMW was conveying. "They showed me that they had no idea who I was, because the surveyors didn't even know that this was my third purchase from the same BMW dealer."

For worthless questions, consider the survey from a high-end hotel overlooking Central Park in New York City—a hotel where room rates average $700 a night. The hotel's thirty-five-question satisfaction survey asks you to rank and evaluate the valet, the greeting at reception, the look and feel of the lobby, the concierge, the restaurant, the room service, the room, the bathroom, the pillow, and the turn-down service. It asks whether your favorite hobby is reading books, taking walks, or tasting wine. Then, ironically, it asks one more question: "To what degree do you agree that [this hotel] is a luxury hotel?"

It can be just as bad in business-to-business contexts. Is it any surprise that engineers, who often struggle to squeeze eighteen hours' worth of projects into twelve-hour workdays, get irritated by a 130-question e-mail survey from one of the leading technology companies? One wag calculated that if 85,000 employees spent twenty-six minutes per survey, that would come to almost 37,000 labor-hours, which he valued at $100 per hour. If everybody took the time to fill it out, a single lengthy satisfaction survey would cost nearly $4 million in engineering time!

As surveys grow to thirty or forty questions or more, the cost per survey creeps up, response rates drop, and sample size shrinks. That introduces sample bias and makes scores volatile and unreliable. But the real problem is that the mountain of customer feedback generated becomes wholly unmanageable without help from the highest-tech statistical programs. These black-box software packages churn out complex analyses that are intelligible only to an elite breed of PhDs. The PhDs interpret the findings for senior executives, who in turn pass along their own perspectives to lower-level managers. By the time the feedback reaches the front line, it is useless. It is several months out of date. It lacks context. It fails to provide the specificity required for building better relationships with individual customers.

Will things ever change? Market-research staffers typically relish the extra questions, partly because of a legitimate desire to learn more about customers and partly because controlling more customer information gives them more power. Survey firms like long surveys because they are more profitable. Companies buy long surveys because it seems logical to ask a customer already on the phone a few extra questions. But there are too many surveys, and they are too long to be useful.

#9: THE WRONG CUSTOMERS RESPOND

Who fills out long satisfaction surveys or takes the time to answer them on the phone? Marketers must wonder, at times, just how many customers are sufficiently bored, lonely, or compulsive to give the detailed answers the company is seeking. But that's only part of the problem. Survey vendors typically strive to obtain a statistically accurate *random* sample of customers rather than ensuring that the surveyors are talking to the *right* customers. In retail banking, for example, the top 20 percent of customers generally account for more than 90 percent of a bank's profits. Yet statistical sampling assigns one vote to each customer. When a bank samples customers randomly, in all probability more than 80 percent of the feedback will come from customers who generate less than 10 percent of profits. The most valuable customers already have ready access to a personal banker's ear, so they don't bother to respond to the survey.

This disparity can lead to poor decisions. For example, the major finding from one bank's satisfaction survey was that customers were frustrated with long lines at branches. So the research team recommended increased staffing, and many banks might well have gone along with the recommendation. In this case, however, one savvy manager probed further to learn the concerns of the bank's most profitable customers. Although few high-balance customers had bothered to complete the survey, the segmented results showed that those who did respond were not concerned with branch shortcomings at all. In fact, these customers rarely visited a branch. They cared more about rapid problem solving by knowledgeable phone reps and enhanced online services like bill payment. They also resented being assessed service fees even though they maintained large balances. In short, the most profitable customers had an entirely different set of priorities than the majority of survey respondents.

Surveying the wrong customer is even more common in the business-to-business arena. In business software, for instance, many employees may use the software, but it is usually a handful of executives who make purchase decisions. Though user satisfaction is one important factor in these decisions, many other issues, such as price and compatibility with existing systems, influence the choice. When software vendors carpet-bomb customer lists with surveys, chances are that busy executives will ignore them or delegate them to junior clerks. Most of the respondents will be people whose priorities don't necessarily match those of the managers making the decisions.

#8: EMPLOYEES DON'T KNOW HOW TO TAKE CORRECTIVE ACTION

Frontline employees, like their customers, rail against long surveys. How can they be expected to respond to the deluge of replies to all those questions? Of course, if they did have the time, they would probably be responding to the needs of the wrong customers.

To be actionable, customer feedback needs to relate specific problems to specific groups of customers—in particular, customers with enough economic value to merit investing in solutions to their concerns. But customer anonymity is a hallowed principle of market research, so there isn't even the possibility of follow-up questions to probe root causes and possible solutions. Why should a company's employees even care to learn that some small and anonymous group of customers who happened to respond to a survey were more or less satisfied than the anonymous group of customers who happened to respond last month? Without precise and timely data, the employees won't learn much, and they can't take corrective action. There is no way to close the loop with customers who make suggestions or who report that they are dissatisfied with their experience.

Everyone has a customer-service story from the personal-computer industry, perhaps because it has grown so fast in recent years. My own is this: I ordered a PC from an outstanding company whose merits I have extolled in public on many occasions. When the computer arrived, it was missing a rubber foot, so it wobbled and scratched the surface of my desk. I called customer service, was transferred twice, and waited each time in a long queue. Each time the representative on the other end of the line asked me the same question: Was I sure that the missing piece wasn't stuck in the packing material? Eventually a rep promised to send me the missing foot, but after three weeks it still hadn't arrived. What did arrive was an online satisfaction survey. I promptly filled it out with failing scores—but I never heard back from the company.

When I told this story to an executive at the computer company, he apologized and rather sheepishly explained that the satisfaction surveys came out of marketing, not operations. No one in operations was accountable for fixing problems reported through marketing's survey. Knowing how well that company is managed, I presume that by the time you read this, its managers will have addressed this organizational glitch. But the story illustrates how even the most committed companies waste money on surveys and mess with customer relationships because they don't establish ownership for customer feedback.

#7: TOO MANY SURVEYS ARE MARKETING CAMPAIGNS IN DISGUISE

Many firms commission surveyors to call customers but have no intention of fixing problems or improving their experience; the survey is solely a promotional strategy. These phony marketing campaigns have helped destroy the credibility of satisfaction data.

For example, it seems as if every car manufacturer has some award to tout in full-page newspaper advertisements. One week, some company announces that it has won the R.L. Polk "Highest Overall Manufacturer Loyalty" award. The next week, another manufacturer crows that it has won the coveted J.D. Power and Associates award for initial quality. Then a third company announces that it has won the award for midsize cars. In airlines it gets even sillier. There are J.D. Power winners for flights over five hundred miles and flights under five hundred miles. Perhaps we'll soon see awards for the highest customer satisfaction among bankrupt airlines.

If J.D. Power doesn't create a category in which you can win, there are plenty of alternatives. One of the large national banks bought a full-page ad to announce its recognition by the American Customer Satisfaction Index (ACSI) as the highest-rated major bank. As it happens, there are plenty of other banks with equal or better customer loyalty, but ACSI surveys customers of only the very largest institutions. Then, too, you can always game the system. Several auto manufacturers discovered they could boost their J.D. Power score by calling all customers two weeks after they purchased a new car to ask if everything was OK. The manufacturers saved money by hiring an outside vendor to do the calling. They didn't care that the vendor had no way to take action on the feedback, because the real purpose of the call was to prime customers for a subsequent call from Power.

The ethics of this process are obviously questionable, but there are even worse abuses. Some marketers disguise sales calls with initial questions about a recent purchase transaction. Customers are less prone to hang up when they are asked about their level of satisfaction than when they get cold-called by a phone sales rep.

Is it any wonder that millions of customers have signed on to no-call lists and that sophisticated spam filters have been developed to guard e-mail in-boxes?

#6: SURVEY SCORES DON'T LINK TO ECONOMICS

Bain research teams consistently find that the links between satisfaction-survey scores and customer behaviors that drive profitability or growth are tenuous at best. Detailed analysis of individual customers, for example, typically finds that between 60 and 80 percent of customer defectors score themselves as "satisfied" or "very satisfied" on surveys preceding their defection. Conversely, companies that achieve satisfaction scores of 80 or even 90 percent often experience no economic advantage from the apparent customer loyalty. Satisfaction is simply too low a hurdle if the goal is superior relationships.

Despite this research, vendors who perform satisfaction surveys often go to great lengths to assert the value of surveys because they don't want to lose their accounts. In the absence of actual customer purchase or referral records, these vendors may add a survey question like "Do you intend to repurchase?" as a proxy for proven repurchase loyalty. But our research shows only spotty correlation between intentions and actual purchases across most businesses. In auto sales, for example, two-thirds of customers say they intend to repurchase the same brand, but fewer than one-third actually do.

Some recent evidence that there is little connection between satisfaction scores and economic results comes from the ACSI itself, whose data used to be published each quarter in the *Wall Street Journal* (under the heading of marketing, not investing). The ACSI is overseen by Claes Fornell, a University of Michigan professor who has been researching customer satisfaction since the 1980s and has published dozens of articles on the subject. The index is funded in part by subscriptions sold to leading organizations such as Wachovia, Kroger, Comcast, and the U.S. Department of Labor. Fornell was assisted in the design of the ACSI by Barbara Everitt Bryant, who had previously served as the director of the U.S. Census Bureau under President George H. W. Bush.

On February 18, 2003, the *Journal* reported that Fornell had been buying or short-selling shares of companies surveyed by the ACSI prior to releasing the data for publication.[1] The article focused on the ethical issues of acting on proprietary information before the public announcement, pointing out that academia's rules about the use of research tend to be very forgiving and noting that, because the information came from customers rather than from the companies themselves, Fornell had probably avoided any issues of insider trading. Even so, the paper reported the next day that Robert J. Dolan, dean of the University of Michigan Business School, wanted to put an end to this kind of trading. "I have instructed anyone affiliated with the ACSI not to make personal use of the information gathered in the course of producing the quarterly index, prior to the index's release to the general public, and they have agreed," Dolan told the *Journal*.[2]

At any rate, the initial article missed the real story. The question it should have addressed was whether the ACSI data actually enabled Fornell to beat the market. In his follow-up the next day, though, reporter Jon E. Hilsenrath focused on precisely this question. Headlined "Satisfaction Theory: Mixed Yield—Professor's Portfolio Shows Strategy of Linking Returns to Reputation Isn't Perfect," the article examined the relationship between ACSI scores and the price performance of individual company share prices, contending that, while some companies such as Yahoo! improved in both satisfaction and share price, "many other companies with high satisfaction ratings are performing even more poorly than the overall market . . . [and so] many stock analysts aren't convinced that the university's customer-satisfaction index, in and of itself, is all that important."[3] Fornell argues the contrary, pointing to academic studies that claim to establish a link between satisfaction and shareholder value.[4] But most investors and savvy managers seem to side with the *Journal*—they heavily discount the results of satisfaction surveys. This is the real problem. If customer satisfaction surveys were practical predictors of growth, then the biggest survey buyers would be hedge funds and investment managers. In fact, investors rarely waste money on standard satisfaction-survey data, because it hasn't yielded much insight into customer loyalty and growth.

#5: PLAIN-VANILLA SOLUTIONS CAN'T MEET COMPANIES' UNIQUE NEEDS

Too many companies rely on the cookie-cutter market-research tools hyped by survey vendors. Survey firms hawk these wares not because they are so profitable or so effective—indeed, they get little R&D investment—but because they can lead to customized research projects with higher margins. Predictably, the users of cookie-cutter surveys end up with crummy data. What they need is custom research solutions to address their unique customer-relationship issues and internal processes; what they get is one-size-fits-all. In an effort to make their offerings sound more impressive than those of their competitors, vendors develop ever-longer and more-complex surveys and use them to generate intricate tabulations and cross-tabulations. But the result is the same. The more satisfaction data sounds like research rather than simple feedback, the less use it will be to management, boards of directors, and investors.

Pat Flood, CEO of HomeBanc, came to the same conclusion as did Andy Taylor of Enterprise; the standard approaches to measuring customer satisfaction simply would not work. So HomeBanc developed its own process: the company's closing attorneys give each customer a brief survey right after closing the loan. Almost 70 percent of customers respond, and the results are linked to the bonuses and promotions of each employee who touched that customer throughout his or her experience with HomeBanc.

#4: THERE ARE NO GENERALLY ACCEPTED STANDARDS

When the new CEO of one of the world's largest telephone companies asked how many different satisfaction metrics his management team used around the globe, the answer was more than two dozen. Each country and each business line utilized its own survey vendors. Each had developed its own questions, its own sampling methodology, and its own grading scales. Some liked a five-point scale, others preferred seven, still others nine. And each division had different schedules for reporting results. The CEO concluded that with such a hodgepodge, the company really couldn't tell who was doing the best job building customer loyalty. Nor was there any accountability. If a division didn't like its satisfaction results, its managers could tinker with its methods or experiment with different vendors.

Such confusion often leads to trouble. A large bank, for instance, hired a group of statisticians to calculate the connection between satisfaction scores and customer attrition in its credit-card business. The statisticians determined that, on a scale from zero to ten, the breakpoint for defection was a satisfaction rating between seven and eight. However, operating managers pointed out that the real driver of growth and profits in credit cards isn't retention, it's usage. Most customers carry several cards, but it is their primary card issuer that earns the big profits. When the bank's researchers reexamined the data with "primary card" and usage as the dependent variables, they learned they had to get customers up to a nine or ten in satisfaction to earn the top slot in the wallet. Conclusions drawn by statisticians with little knowledge of the business, the competition, or the practical realities of the marketplace are often misleading or wrong. Unfortunately, most line managers don't dig into satisfaction numbers the way they dig into financial statements.

Since the link between survey responses and customer behavior is always shaky, debates about best practices are strictly academic. Consider the search for the best scale for measuring and reporting customer feedback. Some experts argue that a simple yes or no is best. Others advocate a 5-point scale where one means excellent, 3 represents neutral, and 5 means poor. Still others prefer to reverse that 5-point scale, making a score of 1 equivalent to poor, and so on. Some vendors don't provide a "neutral" box, so that customers will be forced to choose between positive and negative—no fence sitting allowed. Experts coming out of the quality movement often rely on a "customer value index" based on a

100-point or a 1,000-point scale. Arguments about these scales are waged with religious fervor.

All this confusion is reminiscent of medieval European villages, where trade was difficult because each town had its own unique system of weights and measures. Today's nonstandard metrics clog the arteries of commerce and learning just as they did hundreds of years ago. The absence of a standard, intuitive system makes it harder for customers to report their feedback consistently and harder for companies to interpret and use it. For the unscrupulous, obfuscation is as easy as creating a unique scale and then modifying it every few years.

#3: SURVEYS CONFUSE TRANSACTIONS WITH RELATIONSHIPS

Companies get confused about the goal of a satisfaction survey. Are they assessing a customer's satisfaction with a specific transaction? Or are they assessing the quality of their customer relationships? The former is relatively simple and is best done immediately following the transaction. But evaluating a customer's relationship with a company goes beyond the sum of all an individual's transactions. It includes every detail of the customer's experience— awareness, shopping, pricing, using, servicing—along with all the emotional and branding issues.

Each point of interaction is not equally important to all customers, so some survey protocols require customers to rate how important a given aspect or interaction is and how satisfied they were with each. The problem is that most customers can't answer these questions, unless something surprised them either positively or negatively. So traditional survey methodology rarely supplies much insight into how companies can generate more promoters and fewer detractors. For instance, most transactions, even if

perfectly handled, are not important enough to create a promoter. But a transaction that is screwed up can easily create a
detractor. Customers don't go out of their way to make enthusiastic referrals just because you send their bill accurately and punc-
tually. But if you mess up even once, the unhappy customer may
wail from the mountaintop.

A large bank's first attempt at building a reliable relationship
metric simply tallied up all the transactional satisfaction scores.
Not surprisingly, these didn't tell the bank's managers much. Only
when they began to home in on the goal of creating promoters—
their term was "customer delight," but what they were tracking was
scores of nine or ten on the Ultimate Question—could they focus
on the key drivers of growth. Standard satisfaction surveys were
not up to the job.

#2: SATISFACTION SURVEYS DISSATISFY CUSTOMERS

Most managers completely forget the Golden Rule when it comes
to large-scale surveys. They themselves hate to be interrupted at
dinner, but they authorize their company to intrude into the lives
of millions of their customers. They hire contractors, who have little knowledge of customer needs or the sponsor's business, to represent the company brand. More and more companies use
interactive voice-response systems—you talk to the computer. Few
customers miss the message that the company considers its own
time (but not yours) too valuable to waste on surveys.

And what happens when customers actually take the survey
seriously and register complaints? Sometimes they get no response
at all, as happened to me with my computer supplier. Other times
they receive no more than a vapid form letter. Both are like rub-
bing salt into a wound. The customer knows that the firm is aware

of the problem, because he or she took the time and effort to respond to the survey, yet the company does nothing to make it right. The data gets trapped at headquarters in a staff group that has little ability to fix the problem.

It doesn't have to be this way. At Harley-Davidson, for example, customers are treated like family members; they get phone calls only from recent Harley retirees (hired back part-time) who know the company and its products well and who are charged with listening closely to customers. Not coincidentally, these retirees generate deeper customer insights while also reinforcing the Harley culture and brand. At Southwest Airlines, president Colleen Barrett insists that any employees who want feedback from a customer write a personal letter requesting that information and explaining what they intend to do with it. They must also write a thank-you to customers who respond, describing the actions that will be taken as a result of their feedback.

A friend of mine raved about her new Jaguar, especially the outstanding treatment she received from her local dealer. Then her phone rang at a moment when her house was full of repairmen, including some who needed to work with the phone lines. Sure enough: a survey. My friend was willing to answer the survey at a more convenient time, but the caller was reading his script so fast that she never got a chance to explain. Because he was calling on behalf of Jaguar, she resentfully complied with the survey. But the next time she saw her salesman, she told him, "The only unsatisfactory part of the Jaguar experience is your satisfaction survey!"

#1: GAMING AND MANIPULATION WRECK THEIR CREDIBILITY

We have finally come to the number one reason that customer-satisfaction surveys fail: lack of credibility. When companies link satisfaction scores to employee rewards, employees often come to see the scores as ends in themselves. Instead of focusing their energy and creativity on improving customer experiences and relationships, employees get creative about gaming the system.

Some of the most sophisticated gamers can be found in the car industry, where dealers find innovative ways to boost their scores in order to ensure generous allocations of the hottest-selling models from the manufacturer. The dealers may simply mount an enlarged poster of the satisfaction survey form with all the boxes filled in as top ratings, suggesting, "If you can't provide us with scores that look like this, please let us know so we can ensure your complete satisfaction." It turns out that most customers don't take the time or effort to raise their concerns, because they're not convinced the dealer will really fix their problems. But when they are surveyed, they feel too guilty not to give top scores since they had not bothered to respond to the dealer's request.

Dealers admit that, although they support the goal of customer satisfaction, they believe other factors have a bigger impact on profits and growth. So their top priorities include leaning on salespeople to close a high proportion of leads, filling showrooms with prospects through aggressive advertising, and charging customers the highest possible price. Dealers even get salespeople to pressure customers for top ratings, even at the cost of providing free floor mats or oil changes in return. Of course, some savvy customers have learned to play these games too: they negotiate a low price and then offer a high satisfaction score to get an additional $500 off. After spending millions of dollars on satisfaction surveys, the car manufacturers have ended up with a system that irritates customers, turns salespeople into cynics, and fails to provide reliable scores to link satisfaction ratings with dealer profits or growth.

Even the best dealers struggle to keep a straight face while playing their role in this farce. When I returned to buy another car from my dealer, he remembered that I write about customer loyalty. At the end of our transaction, he turned to me and said: "Mr. Reichheld, in about a week you will be getting a survey and it will determine my bonus. You know the game . . ."

It is time, obviously, for some new principles about how to measure what customers are thinking, feeling, and doing.

SIX

The Rules of Measurement

Maybe you are convinced by now that you need to measure and manage customer feedback as rigorously as you measure and manage profits. If so, the next question is how you develop a measurement process as effective as Enterprise's while avoiding the pitfalls of satisfaction surveys. It isn't easy! Net Promoter Scores—"one number"—may be simple in concept, but gathering good data is hard work. You'll probably need to put at least as much effort and resources into the process as you are currently spending (or squandering) on satisfaction surveys. If true growth is your top priority, one could even argue that you should match the resources you now allocate to generating reliable financials.

When it comes to the *how*, of course, a little humility is in order. Generally accepted accounting principles (GAAP) have evolved over hundreds of years. They are spelled out in tomes that run to thousands of pages (and even so, they are not beyond the possibility of manipulation). We are only now embarking on equally rigorous measurement of customer relationships. So it won't be surprising if we have to experiment a little before we come up with widely accepted standards.

But that shouldn't keep us from getting started. Already, companies such as Intuit and Enterprise have learned the basics of rigorously measuring customer attitudes and behaviors. We can spell out a set of fundamental principles—which can serve any company as a solid starting point. These rules will enable you to get off on the right foot: to calculate your customers' promoter status in a fashion that is accurate, granular, timely, and credible. By following the principles, you can use Net Promoter Scores to assess what your customers really feel. You can also use the principles to focus attention on the customer throughout your organization and to drive accountability for good customer relationships.

Principle 1: Ask the Ultimate Question and Very Little Else

The goal of NPS measurement is to generate a highly reliable relationship score. In most businesses, determining the score requires only one question: "How likely is it that you would recommend us to a friend or colleague?"

That said, it is important to offer customers who give your company a failing grade an opportunity for corrective feedback. Like Enterprise, your company can also ask unhappy customers if they would like an employee to contact them to better understand their disappointment and try to resolve their problem. If that isn't feasible, a second question on the survey can ask, "What is the primary reason for the score you just gave us?" Or perhaps for any rating below perfection, "What is the most important improvement that would make you rate us closer to a ten?" Note that the answers to these follow-up questions are purely for diagnostic purposes; they don't affect the score itself.

To be sure, you may also want to gather additional background data on the individual or the account—and later, once you establish that your system is operating effectively, you can test whether you can add one or two questions without corrupting the measurement process or raising the cost. But be careful! Keep the list short. Adding a battery of generic "satisfaction" questions is counterproductive: they yield little actionable insight, and they will cut response rates. Moreover, they will generate confusion among frontline employees when what these workers need most is simplicity and clarity. The addition of more diagnostic questions puts you on the slippery slope toward a customer-satisfaction survey or market-research project rather than a practical operating system that generates an accurate NPS.

I emphasize this point because managers are always tempted to add questions to any survey. The customer is on the phone already, so why not find out more information? But where NPS is concerned, every additional question carries unwanted costs. A major bank, for example, couldn't resist the temptation to add fifteen extra questions. But the added length made the survey more expensive, and sample sizes had to be cut in half. The reduction in sample size, in turn, made branch scores much more volatile and unreliable. Moreover, the bank spent way too much time and energy debating the correlations among the fifteen questions—time and energy that could have gone into improving the experience of the bank's target customers. If you want to find out more about what customers are feeling, a better option is to build forums or dialogues with specific groups of customers.

"We have too many surveys, and they are too long," Intuit cofounder Scott Cook recently mused. "What we really need is more managers talking directly with their customers, listening carefully, and then responding to their feedback. Sending out more surveys may provide the illusion of customer focus, but this is usually a cop-out for senior managers unwilling to spend face-to-face time with customers."

Principle 2: Choose a Scale That Works, and Stick to It

Talk to ten research firms, and you will hear ten different arguments for the best scale to use in any kind of customer-feedback system—yes/no, three choices, four, seven, whatever; each one advocated with near-religious fervor. But the goal of NPS is not purity of research; it is a reliable operating system. Although we at Bain started out open-minded about the best scale to use, we have found important practical advantages to a 0-to-10 scale, where 10 means "extremely likely" and 0 means "not at all likely." Granted, other scales seem to work: Enterprise has achieved outstanding success with its 5-point scale, and eBay's well-regarded feedback system utilizes a 3-point rating system (positive, neutral, negative). But the 0-to-10 scale has many significant advantages:

- Customers find that the scale makes intuitive sense, probably because of their experience with grades in school. They quickly grasp that a 10 or 9 corresponds to an A or A–, an 8 or 7 represents the adequate performance of a B or C, and 6 or below is a failing grade. Even in countries such as Germany, where school grading is different, the 0-to-10 system seems to work effectively. Employees, too, have spent years in the classroom. They can relate easily to these scores, and they don't need a course in statistics to interpret them.

- Most of the world already uses the metric system for commerce and trade, not because the meter is a magical unit but because the decimal system works best for us ten-digited humans. So most cultures and most people already think in units of ten. Everybody knows what it means when an Olympic gymnast, for example, scores a "perfect 10."

• Customers who believe there is always room for improvement may refuse to give anybody a perfect score, regardless of how delighted they are. The "9" response offers an alternative that avoids pushing them into the passive category. Also, it's an early warning whenever a 10 drops to a 9 on a subsequent survey.

• No matter how carefully the survey is constructed, some customers will transpose the top and bottom on a 1-to-10 scale: they will score a one when they really mean a ten since "number one" typically means the best. This confusion rarely occurs with a 0-to-10 scale, since 0 always represents the lowest score.

• While scales with fewer points can work—as they do at eBay and Enterprise—they seem more susceptible to grade inflation, which hides important distinctions in relationship quality. Note that with eBay's 3-point scale of positive, neutral, and negative, the threshold to be listed as a PowerSeller is 98 percent positive ratings. It's not clear that a positive ranking on this scale is enough to define a real promoter.

• Finally, the 0-to-10 standard is being adopted by many of the world's leading companies, including General Electric, American Express, Allianz, Intuit, and the publishers of the *Wall Street Journal*. Satmetrix and Bain have had great success utilizing the scale for numerous clients all around the world, and companies that adopt this standard will find it easier to compare themselves to our growing database of best practices. Standard scales will advance relationship management just as standard accounting rules advanced the management of financial performance.

But the most important message about scales is to pick the one that works best in your business. The best way to tell if your scale works is to test whether it is accurately segmenting your customers into promoters, passives, and detractors, consistent with their behaviors. Once a scale meets this test, you can establish one consistent standard for every NPS survey in all of your business lines and geographic regions.

Principle 3: Aim for High Response Rates from the Right Customers

While it would be ideal to gather feedback from all your customers, it's wise to begin with the customers you care most about—your core customers. This makes good business sense anyway. Your core customers are those who are the most profitable and whom you would most like to become promoters. When you segment customers in this way, you can develop appropriate and economically rational strategies to improve relationships with them. For example, many retail banks are now struggling to retain and better serve their most profitable customers. But can they afford to make the necessary investments? If they focus only on generic feedback—typically dominated by the voices of marginally profitable customers—they may conclude that major investments are unaffordable. But when they segment their customers by profitability, they typically find that there is considerable margin for investment to enhance the experience of high-value patrons.

The goal of NPS surveying, remember, isn't just to determine attitudes; it's to determine hard, quantifiable behaviors. You want to know precisely how many customers are promoters, detractors, and passives, and how those numbers vary over time. So you can't rely on a small sampling of customers; you need large samples or, better yet, a complete census. You also need high response rates to ensure reliability. At Enterprise, the response rate for customers who pick up the phone exceeds 95 percent. HomeBanc's post-transaction questionnaire generates response rates close to 70 percent. A good rule of thumb is this: if your survey response rates are lower than 65 percent, you are not hearing from enough customers.

In business-to-business situations, it can be particularly difficult to get enough responses from the right customers. You have to poll multiple decision makers and others who influence purchases. The best approach is to recruit one individual employee in your customer's shop to identify the appropriate mix of executive and frontline respondents. This "quarterback" can ensure that updated contact information is available as people change jobs and responsibilities. Simply blasting out phone calls or e-mails to a random customer list may be good enough for some research projects, but it can't provide the foundation for trustworthy Net Promoter Scores. Again, a high response rate is evidence of a reliable process. In fact, some companies rate every nonrespondent as a detractor, since the choice not to invest the time to answer a brief survey indicates a flawed relationship.

But avoid the use of gimmicks to increase your response rates—they're apt to introduce bias. One major U.S. newspaper encouraged survey responses by offering to extend readers' subscriptions for a month. Based on the results from this survey, the newspaper concluded that its NPS was by far the best among all its competitors. But when the paper later commissioned an anonymous third-party survey, its NPS dropped ten points. Eventually the paper realized that the first set of responses was biased by its

offer. Respondents weren't anonymous, and that fact alone probably drove rates upward. (People are often reluctant to voice negative opinions on the record.) The nature of the incentive didn't
help, either: obviously, a subscription extension appeals more to
promoters than detractors.

Principle 4: Report Relationship Data as Frequently as Financial Data

A well-known high-tech company flaunts its annual customer-
satisfaction survey as evidence of its commitment to good customer relationships. The company blasts out an eighty-question
e-mail to thousands of customers each spring. By summer, most of
the results have been tabulated and reported. Employee bonuses,
from the CEO all the way down to service reps, are linked to these
results—but the bonuses aren't paid until the end of the year! During this same twelve-month period, of course, the company prepares twelve monthly sales plans and profit budgets, along with
four quarterly reports that are carefully calculated and widely
speculated upon by Wall Street. Everybody in the company knows
that serving customers is an important ingredient for success, but
the customer-survey score gets attention for maybe one of the
fifty-two weeks in a year. The other fifty-one weeks, the company's
focus is on the shorter-cycle financial metrics.

So it is with NPS. If you measure it only once a year or once a
quarter, nobody will pay attention except when the results come
out; the rest of the time they will focus on profit. Indeed, if you
don't develop an NPS measurement process that is just as timely as
your financial measurements, employees will dismiss it as one
more here-today, gone-tomorrow corporate initiative.

Timely measurement has another big advantage: the more
often the reports come out, the more chances there are to try out
new approaches and tactics to see if these changes improve out-

comes. We saw that Enterprise's more than 6,000 branches and twelve reporting periods add up to more than 72,000 possible experiments. There would be only 6,000-plus experiments if the analysis of outcomes were generated only once a year. Were annual scores tracked only for the five countries the company operates in, there would be only five.

It may be hard for your business to create a continuous flow of feedback, maybe because customer transactions are infrequent or because groups of customers historically have objected to frequent surveys. But don't stop trying. Few customers refuse to answer just one or two questions. Survey requests can be sprinkled throughout the year rather than blasted out en masse. And it's relatively simple to generate Net Promoter Scores by adding the "would recommend" question to any other questionnaires you already employ to manage such transactions as calls to customer service.

Principle 5: The More Granular the Data, the More Accountable the Employees

Imagine how helpless a physician would feel if he or she could gauge only the average blood pressure of all the patients in the practice, rather than the blood pressure of each individual. Imagine how powerless a police officer would feel if radar tracked the average speed of all cars on the road, but not the speed of an individual car. Businesses learned this lesson a long time ago for financial metrics. Companies don't measure profit only at the corporate level; they break it down by business, product line, geographic region, plant, store, and so on. Granular performance measurements enable individuals and small teams to make better decisions and to be held responsible for the results.

Net Promoter metrics require the same kind of precision and granularity. NPS has to be viewed as an operating management

tool, not as market research. Line management has to take ownership of the tool and must be held accountable for using it to
improve performance. At Enterprise, the crucial breakthrough was
pushing the measurement of customer loyalty down to the branch
level. The very specificity of the data both allowed and encouraged
employees to be much more responsive to customer feedback.

In most companies, of course, granular measurement isn't
easy. Many different departments influence a customer's overall
experience and therefore his or her loyalty. For example, an insurance client interacts with the agent, with billing, with claims, and
maybe even with underwriting. At Intuit, senior leaders realized
early on that accurate evaluation of its customers' experience had
to include customer service, tech support, software design, sales
and marketing, and engineering.

The trick is to distinguish between a customer's satisfaction
with a specific interaction, such as a call to customer service, and
his or her loyalty to the overall relationship. On the service front,
for example, a company might ask a sample of its customers two
questions immediately after a phone interaction: "Did we resolve
all of the problems you called about?" and "Would you recommend
us to a friend or colleague?" Tracking NPS at each interaction
would enable managers to spot trends or emerging problems; it
would also help them identify which departments and individual
reps were doing the best job of turning customers into promoters,
and to reward stellar employees accordingly. On the relationships
front, the company could continue to sample its broader customer
base, asking just the "would recommend" question. Ideally, the
combination of data would allow managers to summarize results
by customer segment, customer profitability, and type of inquiry or
service problem. It would also help them understand which dimensions of the customer experience warranted investment.

When managers report that a company already has sufficient granularity in its customer measurements, you should be skeptical. One senior executive at a leading financial services firm explained that the company had organized customer-service reps into small teams and was paying bonuses based on individual performance, thereby pushing accountability to the front lines. But closer inspection revealed a contradiction. The company was measuring productivity (number of calls handled per hour) for each rep, but it captured customer feedback only at an aggregate level—for an entire shift of 150 employees. So the "customer" portion of a rep's bonuses was based on an average score for the entire shift. Trouble was, workers on the same shift didn't know each other and had no incentive to collaborate on problems or to invest in coaching and development. Employees naturally focused on the only thing they could influence individually—their own productivity.

Another challenge for many companies is that teams frequently regroup. In a hospital, for example, a single patient may interact with a case manager; professionals in nutrition, oncology, anesthesiology, physical therapy, and radiology; multiple nursing shifts; and administrative services. What's more, each department assigns different staff to each patient. So how can you track the effectiveness of small teams that form around each customer? You can't ask a patient to fill out a survey after each blood test or radiation treatment.

Cancer Treatment Centers of America (CTCA), a chain of specialized oncology hospitals, came up with a clever solution to this problem. It is reworking its patient-care tracking system to register which departments and which employees from each department touch each patient. Scores are gathered from the patient and, when appropriate, from the family caregiver at the end of each hospital stay. The methodology will allow CTCA to compute an NPS for every department and every staff member just as sports teams collect statistics to measure each player's contribution. In basketball, the point differential compares the team's points-for and points-against when the player is on the floor with the same numbers when he or she is on the bench. In hockey, teams carefully track goals for and against while the player is on the ice. A hospital can rank teams and individual members by an NPS that is the average of all the patients they have served.

Every department can benefit from this kind of feedback. For example, it will be possible to determine which staff oncologists are generating the most enthusiastic patients and promoters. Since referrals are vital to the success of the institution, these exemplars merit careful observation so their practices can be documented for training other staff physicians. By focusing both frontline and board-member attention on delighting patients, CTCA has achieved eye-popping results, with its internal survey reporting NPS percentages in the low 90 percent range. Steve Bonner, president and CEO of CTCA, explains it this way: "The move toward operationalizing NPS is allowing us to remove the complexity associated with measuring and managing customer loyalty. The results look promising for extending our track record of four consecutive years of double-digit revenue growth in a mature industry."

Principle 6: Audit to Ensure Accuracy and Freedom from Bias

Ironically, the more progress you make toward granular accountability, the more difficult it becomes to gather honest and candid feedback from your customers. If a hospital gets serious about ranking its physicians' Net Promoter Scores, doctors will soon be reminding patients to give them high marks. Linking any metric to employee rewards ensures that the rigor of the metric is put to the test, as car dealers demonstrate every day. It could be said that in business—as Heisenberg showed in physics—the mere act of measuring something changes its location and state of being. But you can greatly reduce this uncertainty principle by anticipating potential sources of bias and minimizing them through refined measurement techniques.

Sources of Bias

Net Promoter measurements are vulnerable to three types of bias: fear of retribution, bribery (or mutual back-scratching), and grade inflation. The relative importance of these biases will vary according to the nature of your business, but each one requires a practical solution customized to your specific circumstances.

Fear of retribution. If a supplier enjoys market power—say because the supplier is much larger than a customer or is a technological leader—customers will tend to avoid negative ratings. For instance, an industrial customer might fear that a negative rating for a large supplier would push the customer lower in the queue for the hottest new products, or maybe lead to reduced service levels. Even successful feedback systems aren't immune to this risk. For example, eBay has found that many customers are reticent to provide candid merchant ratings out of fear that the merchants will reciprocate with negative customer ratings. Since even a few negative ratings can sully the reputation of an occasional trader at eBay, the system generates inflated scores. This helps explain why more than 97 percent of eBay ratings are positives.[1]

One way to coax out candid scores is to offer each customer appropriate levels of confidentiality. You can maintain enough transparency by reporting average scores for an account while keeping individual scores confidential. Even though this complicates the diagnostic process, it helps generate honest feedback. Sometimes the veil of confidentiality can be temporary. Instead of sticking to its fully transparent mechanism, for instance, eBay could try limiting the opportunity for feedback to a fourteen-day window after the projected delivery date. During this period, feedback would be confidential. The company would disclose individual ratings only after the window for rating that transaction had closed, so there would be no opportunity for retribution. Even loyalty leaders like eBay must strive to generate better and more candid feedback in order to accelerate learning and progress.

Bribery. The flip side of retribution is the risk that suppliers may use bribes and favors to win high ratings. Car dealers offer free car mats; high-tech salespeople offer free trips or golf junkets. At eBay, some customers are pleasantly surprised to see laudatory comments like "What a delight this customer has been" right after their bid is accepted. With a little experience, they recognize this flattery for what it is—an automated ploy to elicit favorable ratings for the merchant. Such games jeopardize a feedback system's credibility. If the credibility of your system fades, fewer customers will invest time in constructive criticism.

One way to protect against bribery is to educate customers about the purpose of your system and about the ethical principles that lie behind it. Your customers can learn to resist these ploys and to report them. An even better defense is to educate your employees, emphasizing that such tactics are totally antithetical to the culture of your company. Then, too, you can often rely on community policing, particularly if the scores are rank-ordered. Whenever one person's wheeling and dealing pushes others farther down in the rankings, employees will make sure that their colleagues clean up their act. Finally, unpredictable timing may also deter bribery. When the timing of feedback requests is hard to predict, people find it harder to game the system. A salesperson just won't know when to schedule those golf junkets.

Ultimately, the trump card for fighting these biases is confidentiality for individual customer responses. Just as the secret ballot protects a democratic political system from intimidation, corruption, or "bought" votes, confidentiality greatly enhances the quality and reliability of feedback.

Grade inflation. Some college professors now give A's to more than half of their students. Why? Professors who give fewer bad grades generate fewer complaints, and they don't have to spend long office hours justifying their grading to disgruntled students. Their courses become popular, and their egos are stroked. Similarly, most customers hesitate to be hard graders. Is mediocre performance really worth straining a relationship with a friendly service provider? The reluctance is even greater when they have to provide the negative feedback directly. In a restaurant, for example, when a server asks whether you enjoyed your meal, you're likely to say everything was fine. But if a stranger on the sidewalk outside asks the same question, you will probably be far more candid about the inferior quality of the food or the noisy guests at the center table.

Customers will also hesitate to give negative comments if they don't believe their feedback will lead to actual improvements or if they fear that saying something negative will get them entangled in a time-consuming and potentially awkward follow-up discussion. So typically the only negative scores come from those who are profoundly disappointed in their purchases or service.

One way to deal with these problems is to have a third party ask for feedback at the right moment. For example, Enterprise's phone vendors call customers shortly after the rental ends. Customer names remain confidential unless the customer gives permission to pass along the feedback to branch personnel. A second solution is to demonstrate that it's worthwhile to grade accurately. If customers see that lower scores lead to improved service, they will be more likely to be honest. Also, instead of asking for an absolute score, it's wiser to ask for a ranking of experiences. "Grading on a curve" forces the truth because someone has to be number one, someone else number two, and so on. If this is impractical, simply asking the "would recommend" question helps reduce grade inflation because it, too, forces customers to think in relative terms. Unless you truly outshine the competition, your customers will not become enthusiastic promoters.

Fighting Bias

To summarize, there is no simple recipe for neutralizing biases that thwart honest and candid customer feedback. You must assess the three sources of potential bias in your specific situation and craft an appropriate solution from the following strategies:

- Use e-mail whenever feasible. Most customers are more comfortable providing negative feedback online than either face-to-face or over the phone.

- Time feedback requests unpredictably if employees have an incentive to manipulate responses.

- Make team or individual employee scores transparent in order to enable community policing.

- Use a third party to collect feedback so that customers can be completely candid—and so that the promise of confidentiality is more credible.

- Educate employees and customers about the goals and ethical principles of your feedback process.

- Develop appropriate audit procedures that will uncover gaming and manipulation.

- Craft a simple and consistent process that makes it easy for customers to participate.

Consistency for Accuracy

Another key to accurate metrics is simple consistency. A restaurant chain, for example, was considering acquiring another, and its management wanted to collect feedback on the target company in order to measure customer loyalty. The chain first had a market researcher ask customers leaving the restaurant how likely they were to recommend the restaurant to a friend or colleague. Measured this way, the target company's NPS was almost 40 percent—quite respectable compared to other chains. Later, however, a due-diligence team polled a broader sample of the restaurant's customers via brief e-mail surveys and calculated an NPS of minus 39 percent. This 79-point swing was alarming, even allowing for the tendency of customers to be more candid via e-mail than they are face-to-face. The team tried segmenting e-mail responses by the number of times customers had visited the restaurant, but the score remained only 13 percent even for customers who visited more than ten times a month.

Which number was more accurate? Probably the lower numbers, but the acquiring company could be excused for feeling confused. The lesson is that it is vital to use a consistent process for gathering feedback. You can't accurately compare stores, branches, regions, or competitors unless you are using a process that is consistent and reliable. If your initial attempts are flawed, try again.

Principle 7: Validate That Scores Link to Behaviors

In the end, there is only one sure way to check whether your system has effectively defused the land mines of feedback bias, gaming, and manipulation: you must regularly validate the link between individual customer scores and customer behavior over time. Ongoing analysis of retention, purchasing patterns, feedback, and referrals (as described in chapter 2) is necessary to confirm the integrity of your feedback process. Consider augmenting your routine analysis by randomly spot-checking customer results, monitoring phone surveys, and routing a portion of customer alerts to senior executives.

All this auditing is worth the trouble and expense. Customers react predictably when their loyalty has been fairly earned. One, they make referrals. Two, they buy more. Three, they take the time to give constructive feedback. You need to audit these behaviors periodically for at least a sample of customers, to ensure that they square with the Net Promoter Scores. If they don't jibe, keep revising the way you gather feedback—the scale, the question, the customer sample, the candor of replies, safeguards against gaming, and the like—until the scores reliably identify customer segments that behave like promoters, passives, and detractors. Failure to do this kind of auditing virtually guarantees that your system will drift away from reality, especially when scores are linked to employee rewards. For example, an executive from a major automobile manufacturer confided that linking the customer-satisfaction system to dealer rewards had improved top-box satisfaction ratings by more than 15 percentage points. Meanwhile, the actual rates of customer repurchase had declined. Don't fall into this trap! It is the behaviors, not the scores, that define promoters, passives, and detractors. It is the behaviors, not the scores, that drive growth. NPS is a valuable tool only when the scores accurately reflect the strength or weakness of relationships.

If organizations take seriously the goal of turning customers into promoters, then they must take seriously the need to measure their success. As these rules of measurement become more widely practiced, my hope is that they will evolve into a set of generally accepted relationship-measurement principles that can focus organizational energy on relationship quality in the same way that the science of accounting has focused us on profits. Over time, indeed, more and more investors and board members may come to demand an audited set of relationship metrics that accord with the rules of measurement detailed in this chapter. Third-party vendors such as Satmetrix can provide efficient database management that protects the confidentiality of individual customer responses yet allows trend analysis and an audit trail if there is any fear of gaming or cheating.

If your initial impulse is to balk at the investment required to generate solid NPS metrics, consider how much your organization now spends tracking and auditing accounting profits, which can provide only a look in the rearview mirror. Net Promoter Scores not only help you see the future, but also help you manage it to improve performance. These scores can show you how to grow.

READ THE FOOTNOTES!

To be meaningful, Net Promoter Scores must follow the rules described in this chapter. Like financial reports, NPS reports must also include footnotes that explain the detailed procedures used to gather these metrics, specifically:

- Response rates

- Customer sample size and selection process (percentage of profits represented)

- Inducements for participation

- Survey medium (face-to-face, telephone, regular mail, e-mail)

- Degree of confidentiality (none, single-blind, double-blind)

- Granularity and frequency of reporting

- Link to employee rewards

- Gaming safeguards and sanctions

- Audit procedures

Part Three

BECOMING GOOD
ENOUGH TO GROW

SEVEN

Design Winning Customer Strategies

There's something terribly ironic about the runaway popularity of Jim Collins's fine book, *Good to Great.* One can imagine CEOs all over the world staying up late plotting how their own companies can make the big leap. Meanwhile, customers would be ecstatic if all those companies would just move up the scale from lousy to not-too-bad.

So it seems, anyway, from some telling research recently conducted by my colleagues at Bain & Company. We surveyed 362 companies and found that nearly all of their senior executives liked to pat themselves on the back for their organizations' treatment of customers. Ninety-six percent said they were "focused" on the customer. Eighty percent believed they delivered a "superior experience" to their customers. Alas, when we asked customers in another survey to rate the providers of goods and services that they bought from, they gave only 8 percent of companies a superior rating. We promptly dubbed the 80 percent the "believers" and the 8 percent the "achievers." But whatever the nomenclature, this ten-to-one ratio suggests a startling gap between those who think they're doing right by the customer and those who truly are.

It's just this gap, of course, that Net Promoter Scores can help close. Create a credible, timely NPS system, and you will be well on your way toward focusing your organization on what customers are really thinking, feeling, and doing. But measurement alone isn't sufficient. Just as you plan how to raise your profits, you must plan how to increase the number of promoters and reduce the number of detractors.

This is a job the CEO and other senior executives can't delegate. It can't be sent out to marketing or any other single department. Rather, it's a task that cuts to the very core of a company's strategy. There's no point in setting up an NPS measurement system unless you believe it's the right way to do business and you understand that delighting your customers is the only path to true growth. But if you do believe those things, you are committing yourself to a thorough reinvention of your organization. Bain has found that three distinct tasks must be addressed in this reinvention:

- First, you will have to *design* value propositions that focus on the right customers. That means developing an appropriate segmentation for your customer base, then creating a complete customer experience capable of delighting each targeted segment.

- Second, you will have to *deliver* those propositions end-to-end. Every department and every employee in your company will have to pull in the same direction—you'll have to "bust the silos."

- Third, you will have to *develop* your company's capability to do all this over and over again, renewing and reinventing the customer experience over time.

In a nutshell, this is how to drive your Net Promoter Scores up. It's a tall order, no doubt. But what's the alternative? To be sure, you can always fall back on all the old ways of buying growth: more advertising, more salespeople, more acquisitions, more line extensions, and so on. Maybe you can keep your investors happy for a while. But wouldn't it be much more satisfying to *earn* growth by really delighting your customers, to the point where you know they will come back for more and tell all their friends about you? Wouldn't it be nice to know that you could sustain your growth on this basis without relying on all those tired gimmicks? Hertz and Avis were helpless to stop Enterprise from zipping past them to become the number one car-rental company. United, US Airways, Delta, and the others never did learn how to emulate Southwest, despite decades of trying. Using this kind of approach, newly public companies such as HomeBanc have built a solid foundation for their rapid growth. Established companies such as American Express turned themselves around and have been posting impressive growth for several years now.

In this chapter and the two that follow it, we'll delve into how the best companies do it. Think of the three chapters as what Bain calls the three Ds: design, deliver, and develop capabilities. Each of these elements continually reinforces the others. Together they transform a company into one that is continually led and informed by the voices of its customers.

DEFINING THE REALITY OF YOUR CUSTOMER BASE

Most large companies are adept at dividing customers into segments and designing value propositions for each one. But those that deliver a truly outstanding customer experience go about the design process in a unique fashion. To segment their customers, they begin by looking both at the customers' relative profitability and at where the customers stand on the promoter-detractor scale. Then the companies tailor their propositions strategically around this double categorization.

To see how this works, imagine that you have determined which of your customers are promoters, which are passives, and which are detractors. Presumably you also know or can estimate how profitable each of your customers or customer segments is. With this information in hand, you can create a grid like the one shown in exhibit 7-1. Understanding the grid is the key to designing winning propositions for the customers you most want to reach.

EXHIBIT 7-1

Separating good profits from bad with the customer grid

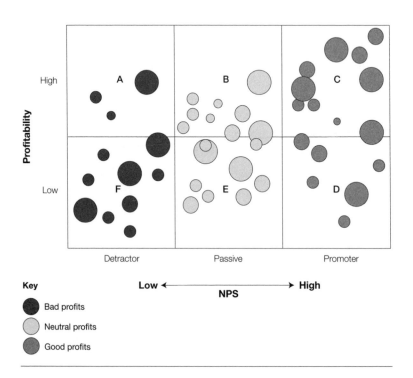

Here's what the grid shows. The vertical axis indicates the customers' profitability. The higher they are on this axis, the more profitable they are. The horizontal line bisecting the grid separates high-profit from low-profit customers. The best threshold for this line is the point where returns match your company's cost of capital. That way, you know that customers above the line are actually generating shareholder value.

Meanwhile, the horizontal axis shows customers' status regarding the Ultimate Question. Detractors are to the left, passives are in the middle, and promoters are on the right. The vertical lines separate the three categories. You might also want to add a dotted vertical line at the average NPS for your industry, or separate lines for each key competitor.

Finally, draw circles in each sector indicating your customers or customer segments. The size of the circles should be proportional to the revenues each group brings in. Now you can see at a glance the real health of your company's growth engine, and you can draw some quick conclusions:

- If most of the circles fill the left-hand side of the grid—and particularly if they're up there in sector A—the diagnosis is clear. You are addicted to bad profits. You have been milking your customers, and they will leave at the earliest opportunity. As you can see, the grid applies the notion of bad profits to specific customer accounts. Any profits earned from customers who show up in sectors A or F are bad and need attention. (Bain has found that the best companies have less than 10 percent of their customers located in these two segments together—sometimes even less than 3 percent.)

- If most of the circles are in the right-hand side—and particularly if they're in the upper right (sector C)—the preponderance of your profits are good profits and you're in great shape.

(In fact, please let us know so that we can invest in your company.) Top firms typically have from 55 to 85 percent of their customers in sectors C or D.

- If most circles are in the middle—sectors B and E—well, join the club. That's the standard pattern. Your customers don't really love you, but they don't hate you either. They'll stick around until something better comes along. Meanwhile, you're making at least some money, particularly from customers in sector B.

Companies that utilize customer-experience-management software such as that provided by Satmetrix can create a movie of individual customer responses over time. Most will be distressed by what they see. Managers feel accountable for improving profits but not relationship quality. So they implement short-term profit-boosting strategies—all the tactics described in chapter 1. They cut product or service quality. They impose extra fees. They find ways to get customers to pay more money without giving them more value. Over time, all these strategies push customers leftward. The customers may still be profitable, but they aren't happy. The goal, of course, should be to reverse that push and move them rightward, eventually into profitable promoter status. Tracking the movement of specific accounts on the grid through time can help make this goal a reality. Sometimes just seeing the grid can spark targeted action. When a division of General Electric analyzed its accounts on the grid, managers developed specific strategies for each sector, recognizing that the urgency and economic implications would be different for each one. Customers in the top left, for example, were profitable but angry—and the division promptly dispatched a cross-functional team to visit each one, to probe for the causes of their dissatisfaction, and to develop solutions. A consumer-oriented company can't visit each customer, but it might ask every member of the senior team to contact a sample of these customers to find out why they're so mad.

In general, though, you want to use the grid strategically. It helps you determine which customer segments to focus on, where to allocate resources, and how to design appropriate propositions for each. The grid can help you visualize and manage what may be the quintessential business process: creating more profitable-promoter customers. There are three priorities for pushing more customers into this category.

Priority 1: Invest in Your Core

Take a good look at those customers up in sector C, the upper right. They love doing business with you. They generate high margins. By definition, these people or businesses constitute your company's core clientele. They may be even more profitable than you think they are: remember how much additional benefit promoters bring you through referrals and positive word of mouth. These are the customers that should drive your strategic priorities.

But how do most companies treat these customers? At best, companies take this sector for granted. At worst, they milk it to fund solutions for *other* customers—those who are less happy or less profitable. Systematic underinvestment in sector C explains why so many companies experience "core meltdowns" and compromise their growth. Chris Zook, a Bain colleague and fellow author, has commented on the historic example of Kmart versus Wal-Mart to illustrate this phenomenon: "Amazingly, their first stores opened in the same year, 1962. Forty years later, Wal-Mart was the most valuable company on the *Fortune* 500 and Kmart was declaring bankruptcy. Though there are many aspects to this story, a central theme was Wal-Mart's relentless focus on its core customers. It invested aggressively in systems that would bring lower prices, better products, and superior service. Meanwhile, Kmart during the previous twenty years was not investing in its core customers, instead using its capital to enter a wide range of other businesses from books (Waldenbooks) to sporting goods (Sports Authority) to home improvement, and even to department stores in Czechoslovakia."

American Express was once another classic example of the phenomenon. During the 1980s, the company took the healthy profits it was earning from its core travel-card business and financed an expansion into a broad array of financial services—private banks, insurance, annuity and mutual-fund sales through financial advisers, and so on. Even within the card division, margins from high-volume customers went largely toward the acquisition of new customers, rather than toward enhancing the experience of those core customers. The rewards programs introduced in the early 1990s—miles or other benefits earned by charging on the American Express card—were narrow and overcautious; their purpose was primarily to limit defections to competitors' cards. The result of all these moves wasn't hard to predict. Visa and MasterCard issuers ate into American Express's share of wallet for its most profitable customers. American Express's growth and profits tailed off accordingly.

American Express soon began to realize that it needed to do better by the high-spending businesspeople and travelers who were its best customers. It separated out the most profitable, let them know that American Express considered them premium clients, and offered them extra services such as a special phone number to call. But the move backfired. The company had underestimated the number of people who would take advantage of that special number, and it had overestimated its telephone reps' ability to handle all the calls. The "premium" customers were even less satisfied than before—they knew they were supposed to be special, but the service they received was not materially better (and was sometimes worse) than it had been before.

Over time, however, American Express learned how to design compelling value propositions for these customers. It transformed its earlier Membership Miles program into Membership Rewards, one of the most generous awards programs in the industry. Rather than only requiring Cardmembers to sign up for it and pay a fee, as before, the company launched products that included the program as a core benefit. American Express created partnership programs with travel-related companies such as Delta Air Lines and Starwood Hotels, so that frequent travelers, both consumers and small-business owners, could earn bonus points; it also created a partnership with Costco, designed to appeal both to consumers and to the small-business owners who are among Costco's prime customers. A special card called Rewards Plus Gold—offered primarily as an upgrade to high-value customers—gave the Cardmember additional points and free extra cards and turned out to be immensely popular. Thanks largely to word of mouth, the Rewards Plus Gold card soon grew to significant size and became one of the most profitable products in American Express's portfolio.

Today, under the leadership of chairman and CEO Kenneth Chenault, the company continues to design attractive value propositions for its core customers. It has expanded the range of vendors that take its cards, even including landlords and hospitals. It has pursued innovations such as ExpressPay, a radio-frequency chip embedded in selected cards so that Cardmembers can make purchases just by waving the card at a scanner. All these improvements have led to a surge of sector C customers who have consolidated their spending on their card—to the point that American Express Cardmembers outcharge Visa and MasterCard holders by a factor of four. The company's results show it: record profits, a high price-to-earnings ratio, and a climbing stock price.[1]

Companies can use the customer grid to assess the allocation of investments and executive time as well as profits and the quality of relationships. For example, you might compare the percentage of capital allocated to customers or segments in sector C with the percentages targeted to customers in other sectors. Watching that ratio can help you avoid the trap of ignoring the very people who sing your praises the loudest and who provide you with the best prospects for growth.

Something else to avoid is the assumption that higher profits from those core customers are always better, so long as the customers don't complain. Because it is easier to crank up prices for loyal promoters than for other customers, divisions stretching to reach their profit goals may be tempted to take advantage of this lever. But doing so is the fastest way to turn a promoter into a detractor. A far more powerful move is to follow leaders such as Dell: monitor margins on core customers carefully. If margins drift upward, either cut prices or use the margins to provide even more value to these customers. That's how Dell protects itself against competitors who might offer its customers a better deal, and thus how it ensures its continued growth. You may want to draw a dotted line across the grid at the point where profitability is 50 to 100 percent above your cost of capital, in order to highlight accounts that deserve high levels of reinvestment.

Priority 2: Reduce Bad Profits

If sector C customers are your top long-term priority, sector A should be next. In fact, sometimes, the actions required here may be quite urgent. Customers in this upper-left sector don't like doing business with you and are spreading negative word of mouth. They may defect at the first opportunity. Yet because they are profitable, you can afford to invest in solving their problems, hopefully even converting them into promoters.

Sometimes all you have to do is talk to them, identify their concerns, and solve their problems on the spot with a rebate or an apology. More often, these customers are offended by company policies that need to be changed. Consider three examples.

- A mobile-phone provider found that many accounts in sector A of its grid had accepted long-term contracts at fixed prices. Now these prices were uncompetitive, yet the customers were locked in—and they were furious. But this was a problem that could be easily fixed: the company simply contacted them before their contract expired and offered far more favorable terms on a renewal. The fix cost money, to be sure. But holding customers hostage to deals they resent, with all the resulting negative word of mouth, was undoubtedly more costly in the long run.

- The life-insurance division of a large property-and-casualty insurer found that it was earning large profits from customers in this sector. The reason? Customers were so unhappy with the firm that they were paying whopping early-termination fees to cancel their policies. Meanwhile, of course, their negative word of mouth was beginning to affect the reputation of the entire corporation. On investigation, the life-insurance division found that some agents were selling customers inappropriate policies because the agents could collect the entire commission up front. When the company changed the agents' compensation schedules (adding clawback provisions for commissions earned on early-terminating policies), the problem disappeared.

• An airline often has a lot of unhappy customers on its hands, but the unhappiest of all are likely to be full-fare business travelers stuck in long lines and middle seats. Smart carriers will find a way to reinvest some of the margin they earn on these passengers to ensure that they want to fly with the airline again. The airlines could offer extra reward miles, for instance, or special access to club facilities. But if they have no grid to identify and monitor these travelers, the carriers will remain oblivious—and they will lose not only these profitable passengers but also the passengers' friends and colleagues.

Fixing the accounts in sector F—the detractors who do not generate much profit—may be a slightly lower priority than addressing sector A, but only slightly. For one thing, most companies will find that there are many more accounts to deal with in sector F. For another, whatever profits are being generated in this sector are too low; they are actually destroying shareholder value. Indeed, given the negative economics of detractors, whatever profits you think you are earning are probably way overstated. These customers are hammering your reputation and turning off other prospects by voicing their grievances. They are taking out their frustrations on your frontline employees. They are filing a disproportionate number of complaints and lawsuits.

The rule for these customers must be this: up or out. Since there is little profit to invest in fixing their problems, you must either discover a more efficient way to serve them or find a way to move them to the competition. Sometimes, of course, they were merely sold the wrong product or service initially, and all that's necessary is to get them into the right package. And sometimes you can figure out lower-cost processes for serving them, just as banks have converted unprofitable branch customers into profitable ATM and online customers. Otherwise there is little to do except guide them to an alternative supplier.

Whatever else you may do, however, you need to stop investing sales commissions and marketing dollars to acquire more such customers. Every ounce of organizational time, energy, and resources invested in this sector is an ounce less to invest in your core. Using the superior margins generated by your sector C core customers to subsidize those in sector F will destroy your organization's future.

Priority 3: Find Additional Promoters

Finally, you and your team must figure out how you can economically increase the population of customers in sector C. Realistically, the two choices are to move the promoters in sector D up by increasing their profitability, or moving the passives from sector B (who are already profitable) into the promoter category.

Take the D-to-C option first. It's tempting to raise prices for these customers, thus immediately boosting their profitability, and in some cases that may be the right tactic. But beware! These referral-generating, positive-word-of-mouth-giving, faithful customers are probably far more valuable to you than profit calculations alone can show. You don't want to milk their good will. Since they already love you, it might be better to find opportunities to cross-sell other goods or services, or find other ways to encourage them to give you more business. (This is essentially what Amazon.com has done with its personal recommendations and incentives such as premium shipping.) The promoter status of sector D customers means they're likely to be receptive to honest conversations about their profitability. Following the Golden Rule, they may even understand that what's good for your company will be good for them as well.

Of course, maybe these customers aren't good candidates for change, given their age or income levels. So then you have to look for investment opportunities that can move passive customers from sector B (and maybe even sector E) into profitable promoter status. There's no shortcut here. You'll have to learn why these customers aren't more enthusiastic than they are. You'll have to figure out what would truly delight them and whether the required investments make economic sense. And then you'll have to track customer migration on the grid to determine whether these investments are really paying off. Otherwise you will simply be stealing resources that could be invested in your core customers, whose referrals will almost always represent the best source of new sector C customers.

Again, American Express offers examples of both these strategies. The company has found, for instance, that many loyal users of one level of card are prime candidates for an upgrade—that is, moving from the green card to gold, from gold to platinum, and from platinum to the premium card known as the Centurion card. American Express has found that the profitability of customers who upgrade increases as much as fourfold—even more for some customer segments. Upgrades are available even for specialized cards such as the Delta SkyMiles card, and the effects are similar. Thus the Platinum SkyMiles card has a higher annual fee but provides additional benefits; it gives their "Cardmembers" an incentive to use the card more in order to earn these benefits.

American Express's version of low-profit, passive customers— sector E—is the segment that uses the card only infrequently or not at all. These Cardmembers generate little revenue and virtually no profit for the company. Yet, because they have open lines of credit with American Express, they represent a potential credit risk. In fact, long-dormant credit-card customers who suddenly start using their cards often turn out to be people who have reached their credit limits on other cards and are searching for other ways to borrow—a highly risky group.

One way to move customers from sector E to sector B or C is to stimulate the customers' use of their dormant card simply by reminding them that they have it or by offering some promotional incentive to reactivate it. But American Express has found a more effective approach. The key with inactive Cardmembers, company executives say, is to stimulate greater engagement rather than just waiting passively for the riskiest of the inactives to use the card as a last resort. One strategy is to offer an inactive cardmember a different product, one that might be more attuned to that individual's needs. Thus an inactive Blue Cardmember might become engaged (and profitable) with the company's Blue Cash card, because of the cash-back rewards it offers—or with American Express's Costco card, because of a preexisting relationship with that partner. In effect, the company reacquires and engages as many of these customers as possible, rather than letting them sit in an unprofitable sector.

DESIGNING WINNING PROPOSITIONS

Segmentation is only one step in the design phase; a company's next challenge is to design value propositions that appeal to customers in each target segment. The key here is to understand that a value proposition is not merely a product or service; it includes the entire customer experience. For a service provider, the experience extends from the time the customer first learns of the company's offerings on through purchase, technical support, billing, upgrades, renewals, and so on. If any of these stages is unsatisfactory from a customer's point of view, he or she is unlikely to become a promoter.

A young company starting more or less from scratch can build an entire business model around particular end-to-end value propositions aimed at delighting customers and turning them into promoters. This is essentially what HomeBanc did. It entered a business with many different facets—purchase loans, refinance loans, high end, low end, and so on—and with numberless competitors. Yet somehow the company grew to become a regional leader, while racking up an NPS above 80 percent (compared to an average NPS of 3 percent in the mortgage loan industry!).

From the beginning, HomeBanc's secret was to identify the customers most likely to end up in that magic sector, C—home purchasers rather than refinancers. The purchase market is far steadier than the refinance market. It enables the company to build capacity while avoiding the surges of hiring and subsequent layoffs characteristic of companies that do a lot of refinancings. Customers for purchase mortgages are likely to be referred by real-estate agents and home builders, two groups that appreciate stable relationships and are glad to refer consumers to a company that provides reliable service. During a refinancing boom, when other mortgage companies are too busy to answer the phone, HomeBanc provides the same high-quality service to purchasers as always.

The economic benefits of this strategy are cumulative. They include the following advantages:

- Employees are committed, because they are well compensated and know they won't be laid off. (HomeBanc has never had a layoff in its history.) The company can afford to invest in training them, because it knows they'll stick around. Home-Banc was ranked number 20 on *Fortune*'s 2005 "100 Best Companies to Work For" list.

- The employees' loyalty saves the company money on hiring and firing, on loan loss, and on fraud, all of which are at low levels compared with industry levels. Loan-officer productivity beats industry averages by 60 percent.

- Nearly all the company's business comes from word of mouth, so HomeBanc spends little money on advertising.

- Customers, for their part, get competitive pricing and superior service—and if they're dissatisfied for any reason, they can invoke a money-back guarantee and get their $375 application fee returned.

Older, established companies can transform themselves in a similar manner, as American Express has shown. The company learned early on that it couldn't just single out high-value customers and call them premium; it also had to offer them value at every point of contact. At one point, for example, the company handled customers with lost cards by assigning one department to take the calls and deal with the customer, and another department to send out the replacement card. On examination, managers learned that many of the calls in the first department were second and third calls, received from customers wondering where their replacement card was or why they had received the wrong card. The company soon reorganized to combine the departments, with a mandate of getting it right the first time. It also initiated a policy of overnighting replacement cards to high-value customers, who use the card most frequently and thus need a replacement as quickly as possible. Suddenly any number of potential detractors—people waiting for their replacement card—were turned into potential promoters, people delighted to receive the replacement overnight.

DESIGNING FOR GROWTH

Many managers claim that they can't design value propositions for targeted segments, because their industry is just a commodity business. What they are really saying is that they have failed to uncover innovative solutions for their customers. Many of the NPS leaders operate in industries that were once considered commodities. What could be more commodity-like than renting cars—the same Fords and Pontiacs that everyone else rents? Then there was Enterprise. And what could be more commodity-like than a no-frills airline seat? Then along came Southwest. If every business these days is a service business, as has often been said, then every company is capable of designing value propositions for particular market segments that can both deliver a high profit and turn customers into promoters.

Perhaps the clearest illustration of this maxim is Commerce Bank of Cherry Hill, New Jersey, which turned the so-called commodity business of branch deposits into a rocketing growth success story. Most companies in the industry right now are playing an end-game of branch closures, mergers, and consolidation, in hopes of squeezing the last drop of profit out of a moribund business. Rather than pursue traditional retail banking, they are pushing customers to use ATMs or online services, both of which cost these institutions less. Chairman and CEO W. Vernon Hill of Commerce Bank, by contrast, stopped thinking like a banker and began to focus on creating a "Wow!" experience for his customers. Commerce Bank's new branches blanket target neighborhoods and remain open seven days a week. On weekdays, they open early and stay open late, often to eight o'clock in the evening. The company's carnival-like branch openings and entertainment for kids have made banking fun. A free (and fun) change-counting machine called the Penny Arcade appears prominently in every branch. But Hill didn't stop there. He and his team redesigned the appearance of branches to appeal more to their customers. They simplified and streamlined the company's products. They slashed nuisance fees, even eliminating (for qualified customers) the charges for using other banks' ATMs.

The bank's goal—"Fans, not customers"—is reflected in Net Promoter Scores topping 50 percent, the highest anywhere in banking. (Branch banking averages an NPS of 12 percent.) While competitors are happy to eke out single-digit growth, Commerce's same-store deposits are expanding at 23 percent a year. The franchise now extends beyond New Jersey to Pennsylvania, New York, Delaware, Virginia, Florida, and the Washington, D.C., area. Returns to shareholders from 1991 to 2004 have averaged 30 percent a year. Commerce Bank's 2004 annual report reveals its formula: "We know that improving Customer experience is key to continued success."[2]

EIGHT

Deliver—Building an Organization That Creates Promoters

I't's a number that bears repeating, because it's a symbol of how much companies are hooked on bad profits: the average NPS for U.S. companies is less than 10 percent. As if that's not dismal enough, there's an even bleaker phenomenon lurking within the confines of corporate plants, stores, and offices.

Not long ago, Bain researchers surveyed North American employees who had worked ten years or more for the same company. These long-term employees are the heart and soul of most enterprises. They're the people on whom the organization relies, the people who carry within their heads most of the institutional memory, skills, and knowledge that set a company apart from its competitors. They're supervisors and team leaders, marketing and finance specialists, experienced technicians and salespeople. They're the veteran frontliners who help train newcomers.

And they are, as it turns out, a jaded lot. Only 39 percent trust their leaders to communicate openly and honestly. Only 33 percent believe that employee loyalty at their company is appropriately valued and rewarded. Only 28 percent say that their company values people and relationships above short-term profits.

But here's the real kicker: only 19 percent, fewer than one in five, can be considered promoters—people who can be counted on to provide enthusiastic referrals for the company that employs them. If you calculate an NPS for these employees using the same formula as for customers—promoters minus detractors—you come up with *minus* 29 percent. In other words, detractors outnumber promoters by a wide margin in businesses across North America.

The topic of the previous chapter, designing winning propositions for the different segments of your customer base, is critically important to improving NPS. But good design by itself is insufficient, because what counts equally is a company's ability to *deliver* those propositions effectively—to win customers over, day in and day out, because they actually get the terrific experience that senior executives would like them to have. Delivery depends partly on creating the right priorities and on sending the right messages throughout the organization. But it depends primarily on the spirit, enthusiasm, and cooperation of frontline employees, the people who actually produce the goods or deliver the services and deal with the customers. If the frontliners aren't excited about what they do for customers, it's unlikely that customers will be excited about what is done for them. Indeed, the battle to convert customers into promoters can be won *only* if frontline employees are promoters themselves.

How to reach that happy point is the topic of this chapter.

SEND THE RIGHT MESSAGES

Today, most companies send a powerful message to their managers and frontline employees: what counts is profit. What also counts, of course, are all the metrics that determine profit—sales volume, gross margins, productivity, and so on. Senior executives from the CEO on down are judged by earnings growth. Store and plant managers live and die on the basis of their revenues or shipments and their costs. Department managers are held accountable for meeting or beating their budgets.

At worst, this focus on financial measures creates a "silo" culture, with department or functional leaders striving to better their units' performance even at the expense of others. At best, it creates a one-eyed monster: an organization so focused on profit that it alienates the very people on whom profit depends, its customers.

Like most things in business, changing this state of affairs starts at the top.

Michael Dell, for example, created Dell's well-known Customer Experience Council, a group that includes representatives from every major function in the company. Dell made it plain that the council would be held accountable for improving the customer's experience. Today, the company has pushed the concept throughout the organization: every business line has a similar council that meets regularly to discuss current customer metrics and strategies for future improvements. The teams focus on innovative upgrades to every aspect of the end-to-end customer experience, because their members' bonuses will be greatly affected by customer-feedback scores.

At Harley-Davidson, then-CEO Rich Teerlink deliberately changed the structure of the company's powerful strategy and policy council, which was ultimately responsible for the experience of Harley's customers. The previous CEO had appointed all members of the council from among his vice presidents—and the VPs jockeyed for position by meeting departmental goals and impressing the boss, not by cooperating with peers to make customers happier. But Teerlink, who retired in 1999, announced that he would henceforth appoint only two of the five, while the others would be elected by their peers. So the prize went to the VPs who demonstrated they were playing for the team, not just for their own department. For example, the VP of manufacturing really did cooperate with the VP of human resources to develop a new team structure to run the plants.

Even smaller companies must make a point of sending the right messages to managers and employees. In Ireland, there's a grocery chain known as Superquinn, founded and still run by a legendary entrepreneur named Feargal Quinn. In an era when regional grocers are getting hammered by international giants such as Wal-Mart and Aldi, Superquinn thrives, primarily because it is so focused on the customer experience. Quinn and all his employees wear boomerang pins on their lapels or uniforms, precisely to remind themselves of the importance of customers coming back over and over.

A few years back, though, Quinn had hired an executive who came from a larger grocery chain and was known for cutting waste. The new manager began to measure waste throughout the operation and in the process discovered that the company was throwing out tens of thousands of pounds of freshly baked bread at the end of each day. (The bread was donated to local charities.) This executive thought the discarded loaves were fine, so he ordered that any bread baked after 3:00 p.m. could be held overnight and sold the next day before 3:00 p.m. Superquinn had a policy that promised fresh bread daily—but the manager reasoned that his order wouldn't violate the policy, so long as the bread was sold within twenty-four hours.

In no time, bakery sales plummeted. "Customers told us the smell of freshly baked bread was one of the reasons they came to the store," Quinn remembered. "Many of them timed their visit to pick up the soft, warm loaves. When they began to find cold bread at ten o'clock a.m., we had a problem." Quinn rescinded the new policy, and the bakeries adopted a schedule of baking fresh bread every four hours. The stores smelled better than ever, and there were almost always warm loaves for sale. Waste did increase more than 30 percent—but bakery sales rose 35 percent, profits increased 10 percent, sales in other departments rose as well, and the local charities were delighted. Employees, meanwhile, learned a critical lesson—that the customer experience should never be sacrificed in the name of short-term profits. How different the lesson would have been if the executive had instead been promoted and rewarded for his cost-cutting efforts.

HIRE (AND FIRE) TO INSPIRE

Sending the right messages ensures that employees at least have a chance to focus on the customer experience without being confused by other priorities or contradicted by some misguided manager. But turning them into real promoters is a job that involves considerably more effort. It relies on nearly every device in the human-resources toolkit, starting with a transformation in the way people are hired.

Consider the fabled Four Seasons hotel chain, which has built a worldwide culture that puts the customer experience at the top of every employee's agenda. It's a culture that embodies the Golden

Rule for both employees and customers. "The Golden Rule has been a philosophical cornerstone of Four Seasons for as long as I can remember," says recently retired human resources executive John Young, who is credited by founder Isadore (Issy) Sharp with creating the culture. "My job for the past twenty years has been to take Issy's vision and turn it into a system. It's really not that difficult, but it requires the kind of consistency that eludes most firms that put profits first." In 2005, Four Seasons was named to *Fortune*'s "100 Best Companies to Work For" for the eighth consecutive year.

Young recalled an episode when Four Seasons was first listed on the stock exchange and the president of one of the company's investment banks was hosting a celebratory event. The investment banker told Young how much he admired Four Seasons and how he aspired to build the same kind of service culture at his own firm. Young responded with Four Seasons–style precepts: "First, you must decide what you stand for, and then you must align every one of your systems to reinforce it. You recruit for it, you select for it, you orient for it, you train for it, you reward it, you promote for it, and you terminate those that don't have it." The investment banker chuckled and replied that if he did that, he'd have to fire some of his best people. Young's retort: "Then stop kidding yourself!"

Too many companies do kid themselves about their commitment to the customer experience, let alone the Golden Rule. They tolerate great salespeople or great engineers who don't embody the core values the company nominally espouses. That practice alone tells employees that the values are not the top priority. At Enterprise Rent-A-Car, CEO Andy Taylor remembers how strong a signal the company sent when a high-profile candidate was passed over for promotion because his region had performed below average on customer feedback. Similarly, when branch managers are caught gaming their ESQi numbers, they're fired.

At Four Seasons, building the culture begins with hiring the right people. "Every candidate, from dishwashers on up, will have four or five interviews before being hired," says Young. "The last interview is with the general manager of the hotel." Since the Four Seasons culture is based on service, managers look for employees who demonstrate the right attitude toward serving others. "We don't look for applicants who can be trained to make people feel important," says Young; "we want people who genuinely *believe* that people are important." The company seems to be unusually successful in achieving this goal. Andrew Harper, the pseudonymous publisher of the *Andrew Harper's Hideaway Report* travel newsletter, comments, "Four Seasons seems to have a better instinct for picking the correct employees . . . something they can spot . . . based on enthusiasm or sincerity."[1]

In much the same way that customer referrals represent the largest and best source of new customers, employee referrals are the best source of good new applicants. JetBlue, for example, has been able to staff its customer-service department in Utah almost exclusively through Internet postings to existing service agents who then forward the openings to friends and relatives they think would be a good fit with the airline's culture. At Four Seasons, says Young, "we face the same labor market as everyone else. We work hard to find a core of recruits who demonstrate the right values— and then treat them so well that they go out and tell their friends."

NPS leaders also try to develop screening techniques that can help them evaluate whether a candidate's core values will mesh with their culture. HomeBanc, for instance, is looking for "selfless, not selfish" recruits, individuals who appreciate the difference between right and wrong and who understand and practice the Golden Rule. The company created its own online tool to screen job applicants for these values; only 70 percent of online visitors finish the eight-minute assessment, and about 70 percent of the finishers pass. HomeBanc actively avoids applicants with prior mortgage banking experience because of their tendencies to revert to standard industry practices. Standard practices would undermine the superior service that is HomeBanc's competitive advantage.

Firing people who demonstrate the wrong values can be as important as hiring those with the right values. HomeBanc, for instance, holds its employees accountable for exceptional service levels. Anyone responsible for making more than one customer a year sufficiently unhappy to invoke the money-back guarantee is counseled accordingly and is typically deemed ineligible for any bonus. If there are additional customer complaints, the employee may be let go.

PAY WELL AND INVEST IN TRAINING—SO EMPLOYEES INVEST IN RELATIONSHIPS

Frontline employees at NPS leaders can earn extraordinary incomes. While the typical fast-food manager earns in the neighborhood of $50,000 a year, operators of Chick-fil-A's freestanding stores average more than $170,000 per year, and some exceed $400,000. After three years, Costco's store employees earn about $40,000 a year plus full benefits—generous for any retailer, let alone a cut-price chain. At HomeBanc, loan officers earn well above industry norms.

The superior pay is a powerful magnet that helps attract and retain top talent, and top talent on the front line yields a mighty advantage in the battle for customer relationships. But how do these companies provide such generous rewards and still deliver good value to customers and shareholders? One answer is that they make a strategic investment in employee training and development, which unleashes breakthrough levels of productivity, creativity, and service quality. As HomeBanc CEO Pat Flood puts it, "Investing in our employees is our core strategy. We believe that the only sustainable advantage in business is world-class service."

As mentioned earlier, HomeBanc doesn't let new hires make solo calls on customers until they have spent seven to nine weeks (depending on the position) at the company's training center in Atlanta. The experience is appropriately called "boot camp" because trainees live away from their families and classes regularly run from seven o'clock in the morning to seven in the evening, followed by several hours of homework. Studies cover technical skills, customer service, and the company's values and culture; students are tested regularly.

Sometimes training points emerge from the efforts of exceptional employees. HomeBanc analyzed the root cause of customer disappointments and discovered that between 70 and 80 percent could be attributed to communication failures. The company's researchers also learned that the best loan processors avoided problems by anticipating customer needs and calling in advance, so that customers never worried about the timing of document delivery or the status of their application. Soon the company was building these communications practices into its standard procedures. On the welcome call, processors now ask whether the customer prefers to be contacted by phone, e-mail, or letter. They explain when they will update the customer on items such as the appraisal and credit approval. Customers today feel more comfortable than ever; their delight is evident in Net Promoter Scores topping 80 percent.

Four Seasons also takes employee training seriously. For trainees, it isn't enough simply to learn or relearn the Golden Rule; they must learn how to apply it in different situations. For example:

- In one training program, employees role-play the boss of an employee who's falling short of the hotel's customer-service standards. The "boss" in the scenario learns that it's unfair to other workers and customers not to terminate an employee who has received the proper training, support, and coaching, yet still fails to deliver.

- In another scenario, an employee who has problems with a coworker or boss complains to everyone else in the organization instead of talking directly with the person in question. The trainer asks each employee, "If someone has a problem with you, what would you like him or her to do about it?" Of course, everyone's answer is that direct confrontation is preferable to hearing about the problem from somebody else. So employees learn to take responsibility for developing solutions to conflicts, rather than standing on the sidelines criticizing.

Four Seasons also has more than twenty proprietary training modules for employees who aspire to a promotion in the company. Many entry-level hires have worked their way up the Four Seasons organization to management positions.

Formal training is only part of the story, however, since the company knows that most learning takes place on the job. All new hires are placed alongside peer trainers who are responsible for helping them learn the ropes in a seven-part introductory training program. One of the segments in this orientation program, "The Customer and You," helps employees develop relationship skills for the different types of customers they'll encounter and helps them find ways to delight these customers.

In one scenario, for example, a well-dressed couple walks up to the front desk on a quiet evening when the hotel is fully staffed and asks, "Does your main restaurant serve seafood?" The first response by the person playing the desk clerk is, "I'm not certain, sir, but let me check." He picks up the phone, calls the restaurant, puts down the receiver, and says with a big smile, "Yes, sir, I'm happy to tell you they do serve seafood."

Then the group is asked to think of an even better response. Someone usually suggests that the front desk should always have a menu, including the daily specials. Someone else might point out that the clerk should have eaten in the restaurant so he could comment knowledgeably about the menu. In one case, a trainee suggested that the front-desk clerk should not only offer the menu to the customer, noting the seafood entrees, but also call the restaurant to determine which of the daily specials are still available and offer to make a reservation. Once the customers are on their way to the restaurant, the clerk should call ahead, describe their appearance so they can be greeted by name, and remind the maître d' to suggest an appropriate wine to go with seafood.

The point of this exercise is to get new employees to think about all of the creative possibilities for delighting the customer—to go beyond a polite but mechanical "Yes, we have seafood" response. The best training doesn't simply imbed operational excellence; it encourages employees to search for opportunities to surprise and delight their customers.

SMALL TEAMS ENHANCE ACCOUNTABILITY AND SERVICE

For NPS leaders, the ideal culture is one in which every individual employee feels personally accountable for ensuring that his or her team delivers an outstanding end-to-end customer experience.

This employee mind-set means being able to think beyond the current job and step into the customer's shoes. Harley-Davidson encourages it by asking frontline workers to join executives on their regular trips to participate in Harley Owners Group (H.O.G.) gatherings. Together with the brass, they work demo rides, staff the show floor, serve bacon and pancakes, listen to customer complaints and suggestions, and take notes to discuss during the trip home. Back at the plant, they are responsible for sharing their experiences with their work group of about ten members.

These work groups have become the basis of learning and accountability throughout the company's plants, and the company structures the factory around them. Each group may be measured on such issues as quality, productivity, attendance, and safety; members depend on each other for success. At times they act purely on their own. A few years ago, for instance, the company introduced a new line of motorcycles. As the first motorcycle came down the manufacturing line, a welder noticed that the fuel tank was secured to the frame with a single spot weld. He conferred with members of his team, who quickly agreed that none of them would feel safe on a motorcycle with a single weld. If they wouldn't ride a bike like this, neither should their customers. Acting as a team, they shut down the line. Then they got the plant manager and called engineering at Milwaukee headquarters, quickly working out an alternative design with two more welds. The line was back up and running just two hours after it had been shut down.

Small teams of frontline employees are part of the success formula at all of the NPS leaders. Enterprise keeps branches small, averaging five to seven employees, while the competition prefers branches staffed by twenty or thirty people. Southwest Airlines staffs its airport stations with teams of ten; the competition typically puts twenty employees under each supervisor. As at Harley-Davidson, these small teams help individual employees deliver outstanding service.

LINK MEASURES AND REWARDS TO COMPANY VALUES

Measures that gauge functional or departmental effectiveness often lead to a poorer experience for customers and are more likely to spawn detractors than promoters. Imagine that you run a credit-card company. Measure your fraud department primarily on losses, and you'll find that some of your most valuable customers are being asked to recite their mother's maiden name to fraud control when they make a big purchase. No surprise that these customers will tend to pull out another card for their next one. Track customer-service reps on calls handled per hour, and you'll discover that they transfer the most complicated calls to other departments. This game of hot potato may keep the rep's statistics up, but it infuriates customers and increases company expenses.

The best measurement tools create accountability not just for productivity or efficiency but for the customer experience. And they do so at the right level of granularity, the small team. At Enterprise, the branch team is small enough to assess who is really delighting the customer and who is helping the team as a whole. That's why "The Vote"—described in chapter 4—works so well. Similarly, HomeBanc gathers customer-feedback scores from almost 70 percent of its customers and uses this data to create monthly rankings of all its sales teams and processor teams. These scores enable managers to keep track of every team's performance across their organization.

It isn't hard to imagine how this kind of metric could be applied in other situations as well. In medicine, for instance, every institution strives for high-quality outcomes at the lowest possible cost, but most institutions are measuring so many statistics for so many departments that they lose sight of the overall goal. What better gauge could there be than the percentage of patients who, as experienced consumers, would enthusiastically recommend a hospital, or clinic, or rehabilitation facility to a friend or relative?

Just as metrics need to focus on the customer experience, so too do employee rewards. Although each department at Superquinn is expected to operate within its profit budget, department employees are not rewarded for maximizing profits. ("I tried that once and it backfired," says Feargal Quinn.) Rather, they are rewarded for enhancing the customer experience. At one point, Quinn learned from his shopper-card data that 25 percent of shoppers were not buying from the bakery. So he started tracking that statistic and holding department managers accountable for it. Suddenly a host of creative ideas were bubbling up—fresh-baked donuts, for instance, complete with baskets of warm wedges for customers to sample. Quinn also set up a contest among his bakeries to see which store could achieve the biggest improvement. The winning team—not just the department manager—got a helicopter tour over Dublin and the surrounding countryside for all to see. Today, bakery employees are rewarded on the basis of the percentage of store customers who buy freshly baked goods when they visit the store. More than 90 percent of customers buy at least one item from the bakery every week.

HomeBanc also makes a point of rewarding employees for outstanding service. Crew members nominate deserving colleagues for a monthly award by completing an online submission form describing acts of service beyond the call of duty. A nominating committee reviews them and selects the winner and runner-up, both of whom receive special recognition from senior executives.

At the annual company gathering, the twelve monthly winners are brought on stage for another round of recognition and applause; then, to great fanfare, somebody spins a wheel to award three lucky winners $5,000, $10,000, and $25,000, respectively. Along with a heartfelt thank you, Pat Flood gives everyone on stage at least $1,000 because he knows that only individual employees who go the extra mile for customers will convert them into raving promoters.

Flood reckons that the company has spent less than $400,000 to run this program since its inception in 1999, yet it has powerfully reinforced the culture of striving to find creative ways to delight customers. The program also generates a book of innovative case studies to use for training and development.

PUTTING IT ALL TOGETHER: USAA'S CALL CENTERS

All the problems and opportunities of creating promoters through enthusiastic, well-trained frontline employees come together in that signal institution of modern business, the call center.

And what an irony it is! Employees in call centers are in constant dialogue with customers. They spend hour after hour, day after day, listening to customers' needs and concerns. They are responsible for solving customers' problems. Yet most companies regard the call center purely as a cost—as a function to be minimized, automated, outsourced, or eliminated. They give call-center employees little opportunity to exercise initiative or judgment. They don't ask these employees to weigh in on customer concerns. Indeed, many phone reps are so tightly scripted that they have virtually no flexibility to come up with creative decisions. Quite the contrary: since their performance evaluation is based solely on productivity—the number of calls handled per hour—all their creativity goes into getting the customer off the phone as fast as possible. Of course, by the time a customer actually reaches a rep, he or she is likely to be infuriated by the series of automated prompts that companies use to screen and classify customers. A time-pressed rep, an angry customer—it is not a recipe for delight.

But it doesn't need to be that way. Consider USAA, the San Antonio, Texas, company that is the nation's preeminent insurer of military personnel. The company could be a poster child for many of the points made in this book. A *Fortune* 500 company that ranked as the top "employee innovator" in *Fast Company* magazine's 2005 Customer First awards, USAA instills the military values of honesty, integrity, loyalty, and service in all its employees. Every individual goes through an orientation to learn military culture and nomenclature, including ranks, service branches, and history. Monthly newsletters feature members of the USAA customer community and their military experiences.

Not surprisingly, USAA's call center is a model of its kind. The company avoids recruiting agents with previous call-center experience, so as to keep bad habits out. It uses minimally scripted conversations, and it empowers the phone staff to use their judgment on all issues, including authorizing payments up to a certain amount on the spot. The company also spends twice the industry average on training—and every employee, not just new hires, receives ongoing training.

Rather than being rewarded for high productivity, call-center staff are measured on their ability to resolve all the customer's issues on the first call. This metric both delights the customer and motivates employees. Then, too, the firm invests aggressively in customer-service technology, such as scanning all documents into a central database and providing reps with real-time access to the trail of customer communications and interactions. For USAA, the call center plays a central role in driving world-class customer loyalty. This loyalty applies to employees, too: turnover in the centers is one-third that of USAA's competitors.

A retired military officer formerly in charge of phone operations at USAA—many of USAA's executives are retired officers—once explained to me that the military studied the link between team size, effectiveness, and loyalty for many years. It concluded that the best building block for a high-performance organization was a team of two five-man squads. At this scale, team members could rely on each other; they could connect with one another at an emotional level; they could learn rapidly; and they could respond flexibly to the chaos of combat. Again not surprisingly, USAA has organized its phone reps into teams of twelve to fourteen people. Because each team sits together, members overhear each other and can learn and offer suggestions. They can also collaborate on coming up with ideas for improvements to deliver an even better experience for their customers. (It doesn't hurt that employees become eligible to become USAA members themselves, so they have little trouble relating to their customers' situations.) Employees share their experiences with one another, and recognize those who exceed member expectations.

USAA typically racks up NPS scores of over 80 percent. Its credit-card division generated the highest NPS ratings of any business we have found to date—over 90 percent. Unlike so many companies, USAA understands that its frontline employees are the key to delivering a great experience to customers, and it treats them accordingly. The company's managers recognize that it is impossible to earn customer loyalty without first earning the loyalty of frontline employees.

NINE

Develop a Community of Promoters—By Listening

Feargal Quinn sums up his strategy in simple terms: "We are in the business of selling an experience that delights our customers."

Simple as that summation is, Quinn has captured the essential message of this book. Companies can't delight customers when they are abusing them. They win customers' loyalty by providing goods and services wrapped in an outstanding end-to-end experience. Net Promoter Scores quantify how delighted customers really are. The scores thus convert vague words like *customer focus* and *customer delight* from fuzzy philosophy into hard, objective strategy. Measuring NPS makes generals and troops alike accountable for the customer experience. The payoffs of raising your score—of delighting more and more customers—are growth and profits: true growth and good profits, the kind that can be sustained over time.

Raising your company's NPS is partly a matter of designing the right propositions for the right customers (chapter 7) and partly a matter of structuring and inspiring your organization to deliver those propositions successfully (chapter 8). Both efforts go far toward eliminating detractors—in effect, removing a damper on growth. But the real challenge is to delight more customers and thus to generate more promoters. Promoters rev up the growth engine. They buy more. They generate more than 80 percent of referrals. If you have enough promoters, and if you continue to delight them, you don't need to rely on big advertising budgets or an aggressive acquisition plan to grow. The promoters will make you grow.

The challenge, of course, is figuring out what it takes to create more promoters. You can't just eliminate screwups and bad policies; that only gets you up to zero. Nor can you spend money blindly, since you still have to turn a profit. Frontline enthusiasm and initiative will help deliver more promoters—but you can't rely on doing tomorrow exactly what you did today. Rather, you need to *develop your capabilities* to find innovative ways to delight customers month after month and year after year. That is how you will surprise them, turn them into fans, and inspire them to sing your praises to their friends and colleagues.

To learn how to do that—to learn what to emphasize, which direction to go in, where to focus your investments in innovation—well, listen to your customers. They will tell you.

HOLD DIRECT CONVERSATIONS WITH CUSTOMERS

A company's senior executives are entrusted with seeing the big picture. They're the people who plot strategies and allocate resources. They decide to focus on one customer segment rather than another. They make decisions about what they will offer customers, and they structure the organization to deliver those offerings. So, do senior executives talk regularly with customers to find out what's on their minds? Not often enough. Too many companies delegate the job to sales and marketing departments, to researchers, or to the people who run local branches. Senior leaders peruse market-research surveys and think they are in touch with the customer. But they aren't.

NPS leaders do it differently. Nearly all of them have crafted ways for senior executives to stay in touch with customers directly and with the frontline employees who serve customers every day.

Vanguard Group CEO Jack Brennan, for example, could stay constantly busy overseeing the firm's $875 billion in assets under management, attending to all his direct reports, or seeing to his regulatory responsibilities. But he doesn't; he makes time to man the customer-service phones for at least four hours every month. Working shoulder to shoulder with Vanguard crew members, he finds that this time offers an invaluable crucial link to his customers' concerns and priorities.

And Scott Cook of Intuit, whose naturally quantitative bent was reinforced by his training as a product manager at Procter & Gamble, puts only limited faith in market-research surveys. The only real way to understand customers, he says, is to talk with them face-to-face. Cook and every other Intuit executive participate in customer "follow-me-homes," where two or three Intuit employees get permission to watch over a customer's shoulder as he or she installs and uses the company's software. Afterward they ask questions and probe concerns. Then they share and compare these lessons with the experiences of other follow-me-homes.

When Intuit adopted the NPS framework and generated a list of specific promoters and detractors, the most effective executives did not commission market-research follow-ups. Instead, they and each member of their business leadership teams took ten names of detractors and called or e-mailed these customers to see what Intuit could learn. When the executives reconvened and shared their conversations, they could begin to implement improvements right away—and they could commission deeper research in the few places where the solutions were still elusive.

Feargal Quinn maintains his own direct pipeline to customers. He visits each of his twenty-one (as of 2005) stores every month and simply walks the aisles and talks to customers about what they like, what they don't, and how they think Superquinn stacks up against the competition. Twice each month, he holds a special feedback session at a rotation of stores, where he invites twelve customers to join him for a two-hour roundtable. He asks them about service levels, pricing, cleanliness, product quality, the new pastry line, reactions to displays, and advertising promotions. He asks what items customers still buy from his competitors, and why. No store managers attend, so customers can be perfectly candid. Quinn and his secretary do take copious notes, which are written up and distributed the next morning. These customer conferences drive his evaluations of store managers and inform the company's constantly evolving strategy.

Superquinn also encourages customers to communicate directly with store managers whenever they find a problem. The stores hand out coupons known as Goof Points to customers who report such anomalies as an out-of-stock item, a dirty floor, a shopping cart with a wobbly wheel, or a checkout line that exceeds three people. The customer who takes the time to report the "goof" gets a lottery ticket that ranges in value from 40 cents to $10 off a future purchase. Customers have the fun of discovering the value of their tickets and feel like important members of the Superquinn community; the store benefits by publicizing its commitment to impeccable service. And everybody has a good time.

CREATE PROCESSES FOR SYSTEMATIC LISTENING BY FRONTLINE EMPLOYEES

SAS Institute, the loyalty leader in statistical analytical software, developed an effective system for encouraging its phone tech representatives to help enhance the customer experience. The 275 reps are organized into small teams, and each team elects a representative to what is known as the customer ballot committee. Committee members regularly report on the list of customer problems and other issues that they and their teammates encounter in their daily phone conversations. They also gather information from SAS's sales and marketing departments. They discuss these inputs, assign the issues and problems to categories, and assign a technical consultant to each category. The consultant's job is to ensure that any proposed solution will be technically feasible and that there are no better alternatives. Then the committee brainstorms possible solutions to every issue.

Once a year, it gathers up all the feedback and solutions it has considered and formulates a list of specific items that the company could address. Around November, these items become part of the SASware Ballot, which is put up on the company's Web site. Thousands of users, representing more than ten thousand software licensees, take the time to vote on priorities for improvements in SAS software. The results are displayed on the site and reviewed in a series of regional meetings with customers. The director of technical support kicks off each of these meetings by analyzing the results of the survey and laying out the plans for addressing the items with the most votes. Then he reviews ballot priorities from previous years and gives a status report on the actions taken by the company. Input from meeting attendees is welcome and is often incorporated into SAS's plan.

SAS execs say that listening to customers is a corporate religion at SAS, but *representative democracy* might be an equally apt characterization of this process. The phone reps are empowered to speak for the customers in formulating the ballot. The customers get to vote in a public forum. SAS management holds itself accountable to customers for taking action on their vote. Of course, shareholders benefit as well. The company's own customers and employees work together to improve its products and to create new ones. Management still has ultimate control of the research-and-development budget, but it's really the community of customers and employees that drives the vast majority of investment spending. Many new product lines were created in response to the balloting process, and these product line extensions have spurred SAS's growth. An example is the highly touted SAS GRAPH, a graphics package that displays the analytical results from core SAS statistical analytical software.

At times the best way to serve customers is to nurture a community of intermediaries and partners to solve customer problems creatively. Open-source innovator Linus Torvalds has made public the source code of his Linux operating system, along with a set of rules that enables outside developers to contribute code enhancements. Google has been sharing more and more of its heretofore proprietary code with developers; the goal is to expand the number of applications faster than the company could with just its own programmers. Amazon.com has inspired tens of thousands of developers to invent methods of extending the company's services. These entrepreneurial community members have found ways to link everything from word searches and MP3 files to online journal entries with the Amazon site, in return for a 5 percent commission on any sales that result. In the same vein, Intuit has recruited a community of thousands of developers who customize Quick-Books applications to meet the specific accounting needs of individual business owners.

LET CUSTOMERS GUIDE INNOVATION

Pierre Omidyar, founder of eBay, likes to remind audiences that it wasn't eBay's first-mover advantage that accounted for its success. Plenty of others saw the potential in electronic auctions. What propelled eBay ahead of the pack, he argues, was its capacity for rapid innovation. During the day, Omidyar would carry on daily message-board conversations with his customers. Each night, those conversations would guide the programming changes to the site. The next day, Omidyar could learn from the ongoing conversations which solutions were working and where he still had more to do. This rapid-response loop between conversation and innovation is what separated eBay from the competition.

To this day, eBay continues to tap the power of community through message-board dialogue. An example is the evolution of the eBay agent. This service enhancement began with a few entrepreneurial eBay merchants who offered to help infrequent sellers market merchandise in exchange for a percentage of the selling price. These experts knew how to take and post digital photographs, how to write the best listings, how to establish realistic prices, and how to arrange for wrapping and shipping. For buyers reluctant to order from a brand-new seller, the agent's track record served as a recommendation. Early on, eBay management nurtured the trend by developing a Web directory, which provided agents with free advertising and enabled new sellers to search for agents by zip code. To qualify for the directory, agents needed at least fifty feedback comments and a positive rating of 98 percent or better. The creation of agents boosted eBay's sales; indeed, more than 20 percent of sales on the company's general auction site is now generated through agents.

Similarly, when eBay decided to revamp its "collectibles" category, it solicited advice from site users. It got nearly ten thousand suggestions. The result was a portal that was well tailored to the needs and interests of individual collectors. CEO Meg Whitman describes eBay users as a crucial component of the company's product development process:

> *Their involvement multiplies the strength of our own management team. One of our users suggested a way to speed up auctions for impatient bidders, so we introduced "Buy It Now," a feature that lets bidders end an auction at a set price. Now 45 percent of listings use this feature . . . We rely on the feedback of our users for almost all changes to the site.*

The message boards on eBay have evolved into a systematic way for the company to communicate with its large community. The company operates a board for each merchandise category. An employee known as a pink-liner, or pink (because his or her postings are underlined in pink), facilitates the exchange of messages. It is the pink's job to ensure that participants abide by the rules of the community—no flaming, no swearing or inappropriate language, no threats or offensive comments. Because they are in the middle of the conversational flow, pinks quickly learn what issues, complaints, and concerns are emerging and are likely to need attention. They report serious issues to the head of customer service, who can then notify the appropriate department head or corporate executive. They are also polled regularly for their opinion on priorities for improving the customer experience.

In addition to the message boards, eBay utilizes other channels to talk with community members. Whitman personally scans two hundred e-mails a day and has a dedicated staff member to code and summarize the remainder. She has instituted a bimonthly "voice of the customer" program, in which twelve to eighteen customers are flown to eBay's headquarters in San Jose for a full day of discussions and brainstorming. These customers talk to managers from virtually every department, including customer support, product development, marketing, technology, and community outreach. They spend an hour or two with the executive staff; later, a group of executives joins them for dinner. After the trip, the group reconvenes by conference call every month for the next six months. Says Whitman: "This program provides us with invaluable ongoing feedback from an instant focus group of steady, reliable, and active users." Tapping the community for creative improvements has fueled eBay's growth by delighting customers far more efficiently than a sales force or product development group could.

HELP CUSTOMERS DELIGHT ONE ANOTHER

The *New Yorker* magazine has worked hard to strengthen its community of subscribers. A few years ago, for instance, the company invested $1.5 million in a three-day "homecoming" event that turned out to be an enormous hit with core readers and staff members. Now held annually, the long weekend includes artist showings, poetry readings, expert lectures, panel discussions, political roundtables, and author breakfasts; it typically attracts more than twenty thousand attendees. Writers and editors are able to interact with subscribers, both to solicit feedback and to learn more about their profiles, concerns, and interests. Editors can track which events draw the highest attendance, to gather insights into how they should adjust their coverage priorities for the coming year. For their part, subscribers get to learn more about their favorite subjects, to rub elbows with some of their heroes, and to meet dozens of new acquaintances with shared interests and passions.

In 2005, the *New Yorker* introduced another process to engage subscribers. Each week, the magazine's back page contains "a cartoon in need of a caption" with an invitation for reader submissions. The following week, editors post their three top choices from the thousands of submissions they have received. Then readers get to vote online for their favorite—with the winning caption printed under the original cartoon the subsequent week. The enormous creativity and humor provided by the magazine's own subscribers have quickly made the feature a reader favorite.

Another ambitious example of creating customer communities is the eBay Live! program that the company sponsors. The get-together attracts thousands of eBay users and employees to compare notes, promote their wares, and learn from one another. The event features more than 150 classes, many taught by community members, on subjects ranging from fraud control and dispute resolution to shipping solutions and bidding strategies. EBay itself, of course, is a kind of quintessential customer community, in which delight is always partly a function of what other customers bring to the table.

Customer communities won't blossom unless they are nurtured and protected from rule breakers, so eBay works hard to protect members from fraud and abuse. It also relies on community policing. The company's famous feedback system encourages buyers and sellers to rate one another after each transaction: good citizens are rewarded with strong recommendations, while bullies, slackers, and cheats are blackballed. Originally, the site had no controls to protect members from vengeful multiple postings, still less from recruiting friends to boost or torpedo another member's ratings. With substantial community input, however, the company redesigned the site to generate just one ballot for each buyer and seller for each transaction. By publishing reliable ratings—including brief descriptions that explain or rebut the rating—eBay can rely on the community to take appropriate disciplinary actions. (*Rebut* in this context might be something like the following: "This customer claims that shipment was late, but we have the FedEx receipt number *XXX* that proves it was delivered on time.") Low-scoring merchants don't attract customers. Low-scoring customers don't win bids. The simple and reliable feedback system makes members of the community accountable to each other, rather than to a boss or corporate entity.

Amazon.com, with its NPS of 73 percent, has also nurtured a creative community, notably by encouraging book reviewers to comment and grade the publications that the company offers for sale. These customers help create a body of content that enriches the customer experience and is tough for the competition to match. At first, the company invited customers to post critiques on books they had read. Then it enabled customers to rate the quality of the book reviews as well as the books themselves. Now the volunteer book-reviewers compete for the attention of millions of Amazon.com customers—and especially for the status of becoming a "Top 10" reviewer. (Top 10 status is a coveted badge displayed next to the reviewer's name on everything he or she contributes to the community.) The reviewers' reputation is established by community voting—and once they have earned this recognition, they have an even greater incentive to maintain a steady stream of high-quality content. Incidentally, when some authors skewered competitors or praised themselves under a pseudonym, Amazon responded with the Real Name program; it certifies the reviewer's identity with a credit card on file or a sufficient purchase history. While anonymous reviews can still be posted, they are listed last and are increasingly discounted by the customer community.

Adobe Systems has taken the customer-community idea one step further. Aware of the potential for its graphics-software customers to delight one another, the firm launched a Web-based community for graphic designers and developers in 1999. The goal was to create a destination site that would help customers be more productive and creative and would also help them manage their careers more effectively. It seems to be working: Adobe Studio Exchange has grown to serve more than 1.5 million regular visitors. Forums allow designers to meet online and discuss current challenges and potential solutions. The site posts job listings and other career opportunities. A major draw is the exchange section, which offers tips and tricks to get the most out of Adobe's software products and enables users to upload samples of their best work. By 2002, Studio Exchange contained more than five thousand files, with contributions from more than 180,000 members. (A typical contribution might be a file that creates a hot-lava effect.) By listening in on these electronic conversations, Adobe can incorporate real-time feedback from the customer community into its product design. One vital element is the rating process used to recognize the best contributions to the Studio Exchange. Members rate the contributions, and those ratings in turn have become a powerful magnet to attract and retain the best contributors.

Of course, it isn't just Web-based companies that create customer communities. At Harley-Davidson, for instance, all the senior execs make annual outings to H.O.G. (Harley Owners Group) gatherings. They rely on these interactions to stay current with their customer community as well as with the dealers who sponsor the gatherings. The rallies not only enhance the customer experience, but also provide the company with a window into the priorities and creativity of their most enthusiastic buyers. Some of the insights for new Harley models and accessories started out as "customized" additions to bikes proudly flaunted at one of these events: at a rally, it's clear which innovations attract the crowd's admiration. To the delight of shareholders, H.O.G. chapters are sponsored by dealers and thus cost the corporation next to nothing. There are now 1,400 chapters, with total membership exceeding 900,000. The H.O.G. structure resembles a representative democracy in that each chapter elects a president who gains direct access to the Harley headquarters team and can influence decisions affecting the entire community.

Another company that has learned the power of customer communities is the Lego Group, the maker of small plastic blocks for children and hobbyists. Lego offers various kinds of support to local clubs and exhibitions where members can show off their creative designs, which range from new urban landscapes to imaginary kingdoms and working robot models. While most of the expenses are borne by the clubs themselves, Lego has developed information packets that review best practices for putting on a successful event, including peer voting for the best displays. Company representatives attend many of the events and subsidize the site rentals for some of the biggest exhibitions. Since Lego distributes most of its products through retailers, the company would have a hard time getting face-to-face contact without something like this. The voting process focuses product development on the areas of greatest interest to the community. Several recent model kits have been based on winning designs at these exhibitions.

In addition, the company maintains the Web site LegoFactory
.com. This site offers customers a tutorial on how to download and
use Lego's digital-design software package, which lets customers
invent new kits just like professional designers. The company
offers awards for the best new product designs; the site pictures the
latest winners alongside the Lego products they designed—and
lets customers order these kits directly from the site.

CREATE AN INNER CIRCLE

Intuit's Consumer Tax Group merits special develop-your-capa-
bilities honors for its innovative Inner Circle program, mentioned
in chapter 2. More than six thousand customers have logged onto
the TurboTax Web site and have registered to become members by
supplying basic demographic information as well as their response
to the Ultimate Question: "How likely is it that you would recommend TurboTax to friends or colleagues?" Then, based on whether
they are a promoter, a passive, or a detractor, customers are asked a
specific open-ended follow-up question. Detractors are asked the
reason or reasons for their score. Passives are asked what it would
take for them to rate TurboTax a 10—essentially, what it would
take to make them a promoter. Promoters are asked what, specifically, they would tell someone to get them to try TurboTax. All
three groups are asked for their priorities for enhancing service in
any area of the customer experience, be it shopping, buying,
installing, using, or contacting tech support. In short, what is it
that would delight them most?

In responding to these questions, customers are shown a
sampling of the actual responses provided by customers who
already completed the session. Software developed by Brisbane,
California–based Informative ingeniously shuffles the choices pre-

sented so that no two customers see the same list. Participants can agree with an existing opinion or enter a new idea in their own words, which others will then have the opportunity to evaluate. Once their selections have been made, customers rank the ideas to indicate the relative importance of each.

This combination of steps provides a two-dimensional look at the universe of ideas and generates a ranking based on the overall popularity and the relative importance of each of the statements. Intuit uses this report as one input in determining priorities for development and other process improvements. An additional benefit to the company comes from analyzing the verbatim comments—particularly the highest-ranking ones—to understand the language and choice of words that resonate most with customers. For example, one advantage that Intuit garnered from its dialogue with promoters was an understanding of the top items that promoters value and would mention to convince a nonuser to try the tax-preparation software. The responses articulated the precise advantages in the language used by the product's biggest fans.

Intuit could then incorporate this learning directly into marketing messages and advertising copy. It is obviously much more efficient to have promoters write the ad copy than to pay an ad agency; but more important, these customers know the right message to communicate. One final benefit of asking promoters to express what they would tell a friend is that, once they articulate the answer, they are more likely to relay it to a friend just because it's on the tip of their tongue and the top of their mind.

This novel approach to gathering customer insight—enabled by Informative's proprietary technology—seems to appeal to customers. The completion rate for these sessions is over 85 percent, much higher than that observed for a typical market-research survey. Also, although the sessions are anonymous, users are given the option of providing contact information, and more than 75 percent do. This enables Intuit to contact these customers and drill down for additional clarity or ask them to provide feedback on proposed changes in that area. For example, when customers voiced their displeasure with rebates, the company could go back and ask those customers to provide specific details. Was it the awkward proof of purchase, the slow turnaround time, or the amount of the rebate that needed attention? Similarly a dialogue with detractors could isolate their specific complaints with tech support and could float alternative solutions for feedback.

The Consumer Tax Group also recognized that the most valuable feedback might come from some of the company's most unhappy former customers. So staffers monitored message boards and blogs and invited some of the most vociferous detractors to join the Inner Circle. Better to enlist these recruits to help fix the problems, the company figured, than letting them go on venting their anger unconstructively. As it turned out, one of the most powerful drivers of customer delight is simply listening and responding to complaints and suggestions. A company's commitment to listen and respond proves that it values its customers and takes care of them—basic requirements for any good relationship. When it became clear that the company really wanted to listen to their concerns and fix them, many arch detractors of TurboTax became promoters.

The Inner Circle has become a powerful tool at Intuit and is being rolled out to other divisions as they strive to improve their customer experience and NPS. In fact, the company is considering how to adapt the process for use by tech-center and customer-service employees. The suggestions from customers, along with their vote on the queue of priorities, would help software developers and business strategists focus on the most vital initiatives to foster customer delight. One wonders, indeed, why every company hasn't created an inner-circle program to identify promoters and recruit their active support.

BRING TRADITIONAL CUSTOMERS INTO THE CIRCLE

Even if your firm distributes through retailers and you don't know your end customers, you can still use the power of the Internet to tap into and build customer communities. Hallmark, for example, engaged Communispace Corporation, the Watertown, Massachusetts, online community software and solutions vendor, to recruit 250 to 300 target customers to facilitate an ongoing dialogue about ways to generate more customer promoters. In November 2000, Hallmark began to test the electronic community as a method to develop continuous communication with representatives from its customer base. The company relied on Communispace to develop the software platform (which enables chat, message boards, group sessions, targeted e-mail, and more) and to facilitate the interactions so that the conversation remained vibrant; if members of the community were not making contributions, Communispace recruited replacements. A certain level of turnover was thought to be ideal to keep the group fresh with new ideas.

Today, Hallmark facilitators have been trained to manage these electronic communities, called the Hallmark Idea Exchange, covering each of the company's target customer groups—mothers with children at home, grandparents, Hispanic mothers, and so forth. These communities deliver real-time insights that are deeper and richer than those provided by traditional customer-feedback tools. For example, managers came to understand that many card-buyers were using humor as therapy for troubled relationships, and this understanding helped the managers appreciate why some cards worked so well. Other executives tap these communities for immediate reactions to new concepts as well as for brainstorming. One exec was convinced that Hallmark should introduce a book series—until the idea was thoroughly panned by the community of customers to whom it would be marketed.

Community participants provide extensive background information on themselves, including pictures of family and pets or video tours of their homes. This openness makes the comments that much more credible, wrapped as they are in a rich context for interpretation. Most important, there is no need to guess at the implications of the data, because it is simple to ask follow-up questions for clarification. Hallmark leaders say they have been amazed by the time and creative energy community members willingly invest in shopping the competition and providing relevant comparisons and suggestions.

Hallmark also used the communities to develop and test a new line of gift concepts, achieving a speedier turnaround than it could ever have obtained with traditional tools. In one case, it modified a new line and adjusted purchasing in the same retail season. Executives compare the tool to having a roomful of target customers camped out in the corner conference room, always ready to comment on a new idea, evaluate new pricing, or contribute creative ideas. Hallmark execs call their online customer community a focus group on steroids.

Many managers at Hallmark, most particularly the creative artists and writers, are not comfortable with statistical research. However, they happily e-mail trial illustrations to get reactions and suggestions from customer chat. They also test punch lines to learn which work and which flop. The depth of understanding that results from the continuing dialogue makes possible highly refined messages. One card might be perfect for a grandmother who lives very close to her grandchildren and is part of their everyday lives, while another card would better suit a grandmother who sees her grandchildren only once a year.

When organizations like SAS, Harley-Davidson, and Hallmark engage the heads and hearts of customers by creating a true community, remarkable things happen to their business. Community members with a shared passion volunteer their own time and resources to identify and prioritize opportunities. Companies become much more than vendors in the eyes of both customers and employees. They become the hub of a network of mutually beneficial relationships governed by a shared set of rules and ideals that connect with the very identity of their members. Lots of executives talk about the benefits of community, but too few act on it. And too many companies still alienate their customers through bad profits, which means these companies must depend on a handful of expensive employees in marketing or product development to generate any ideas for new and improved products and services.

Delighting customers requires insight and innovation—the continual development of your company's capabilities. The best process for generating these assets economically is to recruit the active involvement of customers and to listen closely to these conversations. The explosion of online tools has dramatically increased the options—but there are plenty of face-to-face possibilities as well, as Harley-Davidson and Lego have shown. Almost nothing delights customers and frontliners more than being invited into the tent to make meaningful contributions on important decisions. By systematically tapping into their collective genius, you can expand and nurture a cohort of ardent promoters, ultimately turning this community into your best agent of innovation and your most valuable asset for growth.

TEN

One Goal, One Number

Too many managers have come to believe that increasing shareholder value—their prime directive—requires exploiting customer relationships. So they raise prices whenever they can. They cut back on services or product quality to save costs and boost margins. Instead of focusing on innovations to improve value *for* customers, they channel their creativity into finding new ways of extracting value *from* customers. Some managers, of course, believe they must lie, cheat, and steal to accomplish their ends, often through clever but fraudulent accounting practices. But even honest businesspeople believe they can't afford to be candid with customers or allow the customers into the tent.

In short, companies regard the people who buy from them as their adversaries, to be coerced, milked, or manipulated as the situation permits. The Golden Rule—treat others as you would like to be treated—is dismissed as irrelevant in a competitive world of hardball tactics. Customers are simply a means to an end—fuel for the furnace that forges superior profits.

This view is utter nonsense. Companies that let themselves be brainwashed by such a philosophy are headed into the sinkhole of bad profits, where true growth is impossible. Business did not rise to become the primary institution in Western civilization because of its power to squeeze profits out of people. The genius of a business enterprise is based on "liberty and justice for all." The foundation for good business is the ability to organize relationships into voluntary associations that are mutually beneficial and accountable for contributing productively to the surrounding community. Companies that tolerate bad profits will eventually shrink their way into irrelevance, but not before they inflict enormous damage on customers, employees, suppliers, investors, our economy, and our society.

What will it take to change this situation? Business schools have begun sponsoring programs in business ethics. The government has passed legislation—notably the Sarbanes-Oxley Act of 2002—mandating stricter regulations and oversight. The Securities and Exchange Commission has been cracking down. Well-meaning companies have created compliance committees and have tightened up their internal controls. None of these measures has yet had demonstrable effects on customer relationships.

The fact is, we don't need tighter regulations. There are already plenty on the books. We may not need any more compliance committees or ethics courses, and in any event, it is easy to tune out the truth. What we do need is a simple and trustworthy feedback process that allows free markets to reward organizations that practice Golden Rule behavior and to punish those that don't. We need one simple, credible number, a number that is gathered and reported on a consistent basis, to gauge how many of a company's customers love it and how many hate it. We need one number that will encourage executives and everybody who influences their decisions—other employees, investors, customers themselves—to root out unethical policies and bad managers, to fix problems, and to find new ways to delight the people who buy from their organizations.

In short, we need to get serious about gathering and reporting Net Promoter Scores. The payoffs will be substantial.

GROWTH: ONE NUMBER FOR BETTER CUSTOMER RELATIONSHIPS

Nearly every company tries to grow, but only a few succeed. (Remember the statistic cited in chapter 1: almost 80 percent of the world's major firms failed to meet a true-growth threshold of 5 percent a year in real terms from 1994 to 2004.) The reason is that growth and short-term profits are often antithetical. Most companies can boost their short-term profits simply by following the practices just mentioned. But no company can do that *and* achieve sustained growth, because its customers will resent the company and will leave at the earliest opportunity. Lacking a credible measure for relationship quality, managers forget its importance. They fall into the trap of thinking that their only goal is profits, because that's how their performance is assessed. Inevitably, they begin to book bad profits. That's why so many companies fail to grow and why so many have pathetic Net Promoter Scores.

Of course, some companies focus on market share and assume that if they are increasing their share, they are satisfying more and more customers. But market share alone means no such thing. Companies can increase their share for a while by buying growth, through advertising, discounting, new marketing programs, mergers, acquisitions, and many other means. But that doesn't mean they are really delighting their customers. In fact, the contrary may be the case: market-share leaders often use their power to milk customer relationships. When US Airways was new, the company had to offer superior service and price to attract customers. But by the time it dominated the Philadelphia market, its executives thought they could get away with charging unreasonably high prices while letting service levels decline. Eventually, the company created so many detractors that it opened the door for Southwest Airlines to enter the market.

Nor can companies assume that their customers must be happy because otherwise they would defect to the competition. Switching costs in many industries are often high. If customers have set up their small-business bookkeeping on QuickBooks financial software, they will be reluctant to go through all the work necessary to use a different program next year. If they need warranty service on their computer, they must wait on hold for thirty minutes in hopes of reaching the manufacturer's tech support. If they have invested the time to enter their vendor addresses and account numbers for online bill payment, automatic payments, and deposits with their bank, they will find that switching to another bank is time-consuming and costly. Companies typically do all they can to *increase* these switching costs. Mobile-phone providers, for example, lobbied to restrict the portability of phone numbers. In doing so they merely ensured that customer loyalty would decline and that they would lose the potential to expand their tarnished brands into related markets.

In happy contrast, consider the situation of an Enterprise Rent-A-Car, an American Express, or an Intuit. Companies such as these know whether their customers are delighted and loyal because they ask them the Ultimate Question. As they measure the quality of their customer relationships, they can work to improve these interactions. Eventually, the companies enjoy the effects of a high NPS: more and more referrals; more and more purchases by existing customers; fanatical customer loyalty, commitment, and creativity; and positive word of mouth in the marketplace, often amplified by the Internet.

Fueled by all these factors, the companies' growth engines can run in high gear. These companies can see what their competitors cannot, namely, which parts of their organizations are strengthening their brands by building customer assets. One number helps them implement the central rule of good strategy, which is to know your core and invest for leadership. The nature and definition of their core is regularly clarified by the location and number of accounts on the customer grid depicted in chapter 7.

TALENT: ONE NUMBER FOR BETTER EMPLOYEE RELATIONSHIPS

Today, most employees believe that working for a big company reduces their freedom and diminishes their ability to build relationships based on integrity and fairness. This cynicism explains why so many become free agents and entrepreneurs—and why so many others post *Dilbert* cartoons on the walls and view themselves as just putting in time.

When a company focuses on improving its NPS, by contrast, its employees are happier. They're proud to be part of a community based on Golden Rule principles. Their job content is richer, and they enjoy better relationships with colleagues; they have more opportunities for advancement because their companies are growing. This is why so many NPS leaders win spots on the "Best Companies to Work For" lists. Imagine the difference between the job of a tech rep at SAS and the same job at a typical software company's call center. SAS reps help identify customer needs and prioritize the firm's R&D investments. The call-center rep at other companies is viewed by the employer as merely a necessary evil and, of course, returns the compliment. Which job is likely to attract and retain better candidates?

It's only a short step, moreover, to give employees a voice in their workplace and thereby to make sure that the company is truly living by the Golden Rule in its internal relationships. As Bain & Company grew from a small start-up on Boston's waterfront to a major firm with thirty-one offices around the world, the company wanted to maintain a central component of its vision: to create a community of extraordinary teams. But we could not afford to rely on traditional metrics and top-down governance. Instead, we developed a semiannual poll of individual team members. This secret ballot asks employees to judge how well their team leaders have lived up to the core principles—"True North"— that are the foundation for the Bain community. The results of this vote determine leaders' eligibility for promotion. The process has helped ensure that leaders put as much emphasis on living up to community values as they do on generating superior financial results for Bain and its clients.

One executive who witnessed the power of this process is Kevin Rollins, CEO of Dell. At Dell, Rollins and founder Michael Dell developed a similar tool (Tell Dell) to ensure that the firm would build a winning culture based on relationships that reinforce community values. Like Bain, Dell conducts a Tell Dell survey of employees every six months and makes Tell Dell results a component of both salary and promotion decisions for Dell managers. The handling of the survey is also like that at Bain: while the balloting is secret, the results of the voting are publicized throughout the organization. This transparency reinforces the cultural value of open and honest communication. It also builds in a kind of self-regulation, because everyone can see if the results are making sense.

FINANCIAL REWARDS: ONE NUMBER
FOR BETTER INVESTOR RELATIONSHIPS

In the spring of 2003, I traveled to Key Largo, Florida, to give the keynote speech at the annual investor gathering for Summit Partners, a large private-equity and venture-capital firm that is also a longtime Bain client. My goal was to provide the audience with a grounding in the NPS framework, much as I did in the first few chapters of this book. To my astonishment, James Gray, the chairman of optionsXpress, a recent addition to Summit's list of portfolio companies, preceded me and completely scooped my presentation. He laid out the logic of the Net Promoter metric. He explained how his company's NPS stacked up against all the other players in his industry. Gray even went beyond the scope of my planned talk to explain how his company had earned its superior customer loyalty and what he planned to do to strengthen its competitive lead.

I was flabbergasted: these ideas had been introduced to my consulting partners at Bain only nine months earlier. Evidently the Bain team advising Summit had seen the relevance for the client and had immediately applied the NPS tool to this particular investment evaluation. The NPS data helped convince the fund to invest in optionsXpress.

And indeed, the facts were remarkable. OptionsXpress had earned an NPS of 52 percent, more than forty points higher than its industry's leviathans. In less than three years, it had earned top market share in retail option trades. Not surprisingly, its primary source of new customers is referrals from existing customers. How else could a start-up afford to acquire more than fifty thousand new customers in such a short time? Today, Gray is using NPS to track progress and guide his team's decisions as the company grows even larger, reaching more than 160,000 customers in 2005. Summit Partners views optionsXpress as a model investment, one that has turned into a real homerun for investors.

The connection between high NPS and investment success is logical. Without true growth, stock prices languish. With true growth, stock prices increase. The best way to rev up the growth engine is to turn more customers into promoters and fewer into detractors. Promoters and detractors are the real assets and liabilities in a business, and investors need a clear accounting of the corporation's customer balance sheet.

Some of the earliest adopters of the one number within the Bain community have been organizations involved in mergers and acquisitions. These clients immediately grasped that the evaluation of potential investments could be sharpened with a quick X-ray of the target firm's customer relationships. Due-diligence teams learn a lot in just a few days by comparing the target's NPS to that of competitors and by determining the percentage of new customers who are referrals. Bain is now performing these X-rays for potential investments in industries as disparate as cosmetics, mattresses, grocery stores, insurance, coin-operated vending machines, and mobile-phone providers.

ONE NUMBER, MANY FOES

Stamping out bad profits through NPS seems like a universally appealing idea, but it isn't. An army of enemies will oppose a system of accountability that is based on a single number. Lots of managers have learned how to play the game in the current system; they know how to milk customers to make their bonus. And any manager, sales rep, or service team who shows up at the bottom of a rank-ordering based on NPS will fight against the relevance of the idea or the credibility of the measurement process. Even managers who look good on an NPS rank-ordering will be uncertain about their status and the reliability of the process.

This concern is understandable, but it can be resolved by simply measuring NPS and sharing the information for a number of cycles before linking it to pay and promotions. Most well-intentioned participants should be willing at least to test the process to see if it produces better results.

In large companies, the biggest challenge is likely to come from the company's own market-research department and survey vendors. These groups have a vested interest in maintaining the status quo. Since customer feedback has always been their area of expertise and the basis of their organizational power, they're likely to perceive NPS as a threat. The notion that customer feedback can be summarized in one or two questions and gauged in one number will not appeal to career researchers. Nor will engaging line managers in the collection and analysis of customer feedback.

One senior executive who implemented NPS was deluged with e-mails from his internal market-research group and from his research vendors. They protested that the plan to monitor NPS was simplistic—"based on flawed research, flagrantly illogical, statistically invalid, irresponsible, and fundamentally flawed." At one large European insurance company, the research department commissioned university professors to write a paper arguing that using a zero-to-ten scale in Europe was foolish and that anything based on this approach would be disastrous. Satisfaction-survey vendors have much to lose and can be expected to fight fiercely to discredit this relatively simple metric.

Perhaps the most dangerous enemies of progress will not be those who fight NPS but those who adopt it and then twist it to suit their agenda. Some will be uninformed enthusiasts who are so attracted to the logic of one number that they implement NPS with gusto but with little appreciation for the measurement challenges cited in chapter 6. They may link unreliable NPS ratings to employee rewards and then find that they have inadvertently discredited the entire system. If NPS results don't square with customer behaviors and growth—either because the results are being gamed or because the company has not developed a timely, rigorous process that asks the right questions of the right customers—then the system is little better than today's satisfaction surveys. Then, too, companies that advertise their outstanding NPS ratings will face the same temptation to manipulate the numbers as they do with satisfaction statistics. If this happens, NPS will be discounted and ignored by consumers and employees.

What to do about this? Despite my general aversion to state intervention in a free-market society—we already have too many rules and regulations—there is no question that in some cases, government action is vital. Just as regulators enforce pollution standards, the octane rating of premium gasoline, the accuracy of food nutrition labeling, the consistent calculation of interest rate on loans (APR), and the uniform reporting of investment performance among mutual funds, regulators can help enforce consistent and accurate NPS reporting. To defeat the many foes of NPS, industry leaders must lobby for a standards board (much like the Financial Accounting Standards Board) to determine the rules for gathering, reporting, and auditing NPS data before it can be published or advertised. The rules laid out in chapter 6 would be a good start. Of course, individual companies can and should develop their own internal NPS systems to serve their management needs. But before advertising their results to investors or the public, companies should be held to a common set of standards.

THE ACCOUNTABILITY OF A COMMUNITY

Regulators, of course, can't police companies effectively without the energetic assistance of community members who are convinced that their community will benefit from rigorous oversight. That's a lesson that police departments have come to understand, and it's equally applicable to the corporate world. The whistle-blower at Enron was not an outside regulator, but a community insider. The same was true at WorldCom, Tyco, and many other companies that have been caught cheating. Community insiders must cooperate to ensure that members who break the rules—or who milk relationships—are sanctioned. Otherwise, bullies, slackers, and cheats will abuse community assets for their own purposes and will subvert core principles. EBay instructs its own facilitators (pinks) to monitor message boards so that anyone who uses abusive or threatening language is warned or cut from the membership roles. But the oversight doesn't end there. By publishing member feedback and reporting how frequently each member provides feedback, eBay relies on the community itself to take appropriate disciplinary actions.

Another lesson police departments have learned is that unchallenged small offenses breed a climate in which big offenses are accepted. When William Bratton took over as police commissioner of New York City, he famously focused on infractions such as graffiti, vandalism, and the accosting of motorists by aggressive squeegee men looking for tips. Soon the climate began to change, and serious crime began to drop as well. Graffiti and broken windows are the equivalent of a business's first bad profits. Like crime, bad profits start small—with practices such as dishonest advertising, unreliable service, dinnertime interruptions by phone marketers, and misleading pricing—and escalate to bigger problems such as biased stock research, under-the-counter payoffs, and deceitful projections for growth and earnings. When community members fail to recognize transgressions, they become complicit, and the police force might as well stay home. Community members who ignore unethical practices and fail to blow the whistle on exploitative relationships allow minor lapses to turn into major malfeasance. And the community withers.

But NPS leaders have found that community policing works. If you ask Andy Taylor why Enterprise's ESQi system has not been gamed in the same way that car dealers have manipulated their satisfaction ratings, he'll explain that Enterprise audits the number of non-connects in order to identify branches that are modifying phone numbers of unhappy customers so that their negative feedback can never be tallied. But corporate auditing alone can't control more than six thousand branches around the globe. Taylor knows the central reason that branches don't play games with ESQi numbers is that the other branches, which are being ranked against them, figure it out and blow the whistle. Community policing makes ESQi a credible management tool.

To learn how to build community accountability, leaders can look to examples that long predate Enterprise and eBay. In 594 B.C., Solon, chief statesman of Athens, initiated a radical experiment: he established a code of laws and gave large segments of the population a voice in governance. Laws were posted for all to see. The enforcement mechanism was not a powerful police force but the right of every citizen to resolve disputes in the courts. This democracy led to a two-hundred-year flowering of prosperity, creativity, and knowledge. Similarly, after the Continental army's victory against the British in 1781, George Washington was so popular that he could easily have taken the path of so many previous revolutionary leaders by consolidating his power into a new monarchy. Instead, he gave a farewell address at the end of his second presidential term, when his power was at its peak, describing the citizenry as the real seat of power in a democratic society. Washington's commitment to community empowerment helped America's citizens engage in building a society—a network of relationships governed by the rule of law—that has become the world's leading economic power.

The individual rights that form the core of democratic experiments from Athens to America—truth, liberty, justice, the pursuit of happiness—aren't so different from the principles espoused by loyalty leaders. By empowering their customers and employees with voice and vote, companies like SAS, eBay, and Harley-Davidson have simply followed in the steps of history's great leaders who recognized the creative power of a free society. Even eBay's corporate motto, "by the people, for the people," proclaims the source of the firm's explosive growth.

THE BIG PICTURE

In an effort to keep this book short and focused, I have concentrated on for-profit businesses. But it doesn't require much imagination to see the relevance of NPS to a much broader range of institutions. The best way for any community to grow is to attract the right kind of new members through word-of-mouth advertising, then ensure that members develop mutually valuable relationships worthy of an ongoing investment of their time and energy. This is the cycle that builds successful schools, charities, hospitals, associations, and foundations.

When an organization earns the loyalty of its constituents, it increases the resources available to them, and it can have a greater impact on society. Tracking Net Promoter Scores can help leaders and community members understand who is doing the best job and who needs attention. By rigorously measuring, reporting, and managing one number—the percentage of promoters minus the percentage of detractors among their constituents—organizations can identify best practices, unleash fresh ideas, build commitment, and establish accountability for results. *Every* organization can grow and become more productive by generating more promoters and fewer detractors.

On one level, the ideas behind this book are so simple they're almost self-evident. It doesn't really require a great leap of faith to accept that the best way to grow is to get more promoters and fewer detractors, especially in an Internet world, where word of mouth has become such a powerful force. That the answer to a single question can reveal whether a customer has been converted into a promoter or a detractor may be surprising at first. But once people see the facts, it isn't really a controversial proposition. Any manager who has struggled to establish accountability knows that one central metric for gauging relationship quality is better than dozens.

So why is this simplicity so radical? When you put all of these simple ideas together, you come to the inescapable conclusion that the best way for an organization to grow profitably is to build strong relationships among customers and employees—relationships worthy of loyalty because they are governed by the basic set of ethical standards defined by the Golden Rule. It is truly radical to think that the more ethical a company becomes, the faster it can grow and prosper. Yet the data is hard to ignore. Companies that have earned the highest loyalty are winning the battle for market share in most industries. These loyalty leaders demonstrate how growth engines can roar when the NPS needle moves above 50 percent. By creating vibrant communities in which members provide the creativity and guidance, loyalty leaders show that large organizations can continue to grow and prosper—but only when they use their market power to serve, not to exploit, community relationships.

Perhaps the most revolutionary idea in this book is the proposition that it is at least as important to measure the quality of relationships as it is to measure profitability. Until managers develop a reliable process for measuring this one number, they cannot create accountability for earning good profits rather than bad. They will struggle to see the difference between earning growth and buying it. They won't be able to gauge the health or even the identity of their core business. And they will find it impossible to build communities that foster the commitment and innovation required to sustain true growth.

The growth of any organization is simply the accumulated growth of the individual relationships that constitute it. Partners will invest to create better, more mutually valuable relationships when they are part of a community in which members hold each other accountable for building relationships that meet Golden Rule standards. Relationships are the crucibles in which value creation takes place—and one number, Net Promoter Scores, can clarify, enhance, and accelerate this ongoing miracle of creation. They reveal a basic truth: good things grow.

When Andy Taylor ponders the growth of Enterprise Rent-A-Car from a tiny family business into the colossus of car rentals, he concedes it has been a miracle of sorts. He gives his father much of the credit for that miracle, and not just for starting the business. He gives his father even more credit for reminding his team after Enterprise became the market leader that it was less a time to celebrate than a time to redouble the team's commitment to better customer relationships. When his team learned how to track the one number that measured how well they were treating customers, they dramatically boosted the company's growth. They changed the future.

"That one number," says Taylor, "became more than a metric—it became a journey to the truth."

The Linkage Between NPS and Growth

In the following charts, we show simple linear correlations between growth and NPS to keep the argument simple and intuitive. However, to be precise, the correct specification in our model is that relative growth is a function of ln(delta NPS). This will boost R-squares substantially. The size of each circle in the charts is proportional to that company's revenues from customers in the segment.

FIGURE A-1

Wintel personal computers

Three-year shipment growth (1999–2002)

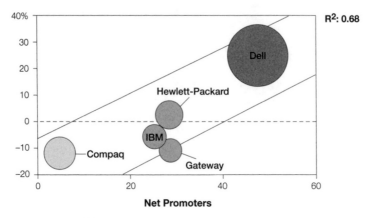

Source: Satmetrix NPS survey (Q1 2001–Q4 2002); company annual report.

FIGURE A-2

U.S. life insurance industry

Growth in ordinary life premiums (1999–2003)

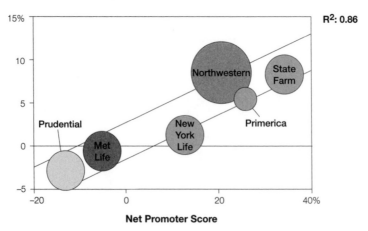

Source: AM Best, Satmetrix survey (Q1 2001–Q4 2002).

FIGURE A-3

Korean auto insurance

Two-year revenue growth rate (2001–2003)

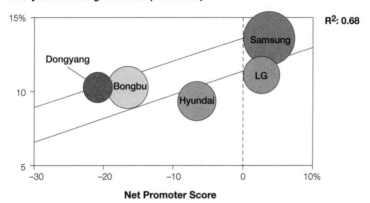

Source: Company IR report, Samsung security, Kyobo security, Hyundai security, Bain Customer loyalty survey Oct 2003.

Note: Premium revenue as of March 31 of each year.

FIGURE A-4

Airlines

Three-year growth (1999–2002)

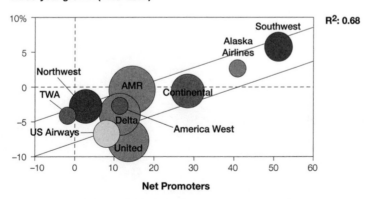

Source: Satmetrix NPS survey (Q1 2000–Q4 2002); company annual report.

Note: AMR purchased TWA in 1999. Used historical TWA CAGR for 2000 and AMR CAGR for 2000–2002.

FIGURE A-5

ISP

Three-year growth (1999–2002)

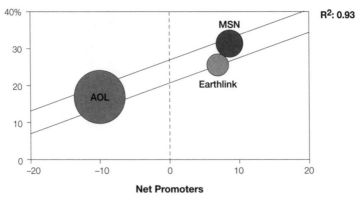

Source: Satmetrix NPS survey (Q1–Q4, 2002); company annual report.

FIGURE A-6

U.K. supermarkets

Growth in revenues (1999–2003)

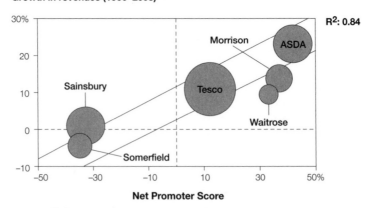

Source: BVD Fame, annual reports, Bain net promoter survey.

Note: Morrison revenue growth does not include Safeway figures, as the full merger only took place in 2004.

Winners and Sinners for Selected U.S. and U.K. Industries

In this appendix, we list what we call *winners* (highest percentage of promoters) and *sinners* (highest percentage of detractors) for a variety of industries where data is available. Usually this book looks at Net Promoter Score, which subtracts the percentage of detractors from the percentage of promoters. Here, however, we are separating the two components of NPS, and the variations in performance are even more striking. While the names of the sinners have been kept anonymous here, an updated list of specific sinners and winners is available at the Web site netpromoter.com.

U.S. Industries	Winners—Companies (highest % of promoters)	Sinners—Companies Anonymous (highest % of detractors)
	%	%
Airlines	Southwest, 60	Anonymous, 34
Car Rentals	Enterprise, 53	Anonymous, 28
		Anonymous, 28
Car Brands	Saturn, 74	Anonymous, 49
Full-Service Brokerage Firms	A.G. Edwards , 64	Anonymous, 36
Retail Banks	Commerce Bank , 66	Anonymous, 45
		Anonymous, 57
Mobile Phone Services	SBC, 42	Anonymous, 56
Credit Cards	USAA, 94	Anonymous, 55
Wintel PCs	Dell, 62	Anonymous, 33
Health Insurance	AFLAC, 47	Anonymous, 60
Life Insurance	USAA, 72	Anonymous, 50
		Anonymous, 49
Property and Casualty Insurance	USAA, 83	Anonymous, 40
Shipping/Delivery	FedEx, 66	Anonymous, 22
Department Stores*	Target, 59	Anonymous, 55
Do-It-Yourself Stores*	True Value, 70	Anonymous, 50
Drug Stores*	Walgreens, 55	Anonymous, 54
Supermarkets*	Costco, 81	Anonymous, 28
U.K. Industries		
Retail Banks	Cahoot, 75	Anonymous, 45
	First Direct, 74	Anonymous, 44
		Anonymous, 43
Mobile Phone Services	Virgin Mobile, 61	Anonymous, 38
Home Gas & Electricity*	Scottish Power, 20	Anonymous, 92
Car Rentals*	Enterprise, 50	Anonymous, 49
Department Stores*	John Lewis, 55	Anonymous, 51
Do-It-Yourself Stores*	B&Q, 35	Anonymous, 56
Pharmacy*	Superdrug, 37	Anonymous, 31
Supermarkets*	Morrison, 57	Anonymous, 51
Credit Cards*	HSBC, 42	Anonymous, 64
Life Insurance*	Standard Life, 23	Anonymous, 85
Mortgages*	HSBC, 36	Anonymous, 66
Men's Razors*	Gillette, 42	Anonymous, 53
Sports Footwear*	Puma, 49	Anonymous, 42

Note: Asterisks represent data from a Bain-sponsored survey performed in the fourth quarter of 2004; otherwise, numbers are from a Satmetrix database built between the first quarter of 2001 and the first quarter of 2005. Whenever more than one company is listed in a category, the companies' scores were not statistically different from one another.

NOTES

All quotations not otherwise cited are from interviews conducted by the author or personal communications sent to the author.

Chapter 1

1. The Bain study examined the 2,780 companies in the G-7 countries that have annual sales greater than $500 million; it found that only 22 percent grew both revenue and earnings at least 5 percent (after inflation) while meeting their cost of capital. Eliminating the cost-of-capital constraint increases the proportion of qualifying firms to 29 percent. But true growth requires that returns match or exceed capital costs. If returns aren't higher than that threshold, growth merely means squandering shareholder funds on the unsustainable purchase of nominal revenues.

2. Randall Stross, "Why Time Warner Has Fallen in Love with AOL, Again," *New York Times*, September 25, 2005.

3. "Online Extra: Jeff Bezos on Word-of-Mouth Power," *BusinessWeek Online*, August 2, 2004.

4. See eBay's Web site: http://pages.ebay.com/community/people/ values.html.

5. Adam Cohen, "Coffee with Pierre," *Time*, December 27, 1999.

Chapter 3

1. The data includes only companies that make so-called Wintel computers. We decided against including Apple Computer, Inc., because of the difficulty of separating out the Apple iPod effect. Still, Apple's recent growth surge is consistent with the company's outstanding NPS.

2. The results of this survey, conducted in late 2004, are not identical to the scores in the Satmetrix database; the latter contains several years of customer feedback.

3. For the analytically inclined, the Net Promoter delta is the best predictor of relative growth in most industries. For more details on the statistics involved, see the appendix.

Chapter 4

1. This account draws heavily on Andy Taylor, "Top box: Rediscovering customer satisfaction," *Business Horizons*, September–October 2003, pp. 3–14. All quotes are taken from this article unless otherwise noted.

2. Kemp Powers, "How We Got Started—Andy Taylor, Enterprise Rent-A-Car," *Fortune Small Business*, September 1, 2004.

Chapter 5

1. Jon E. Hilsenrath and Dan Morse, "Researcher Uses Index to Buy, Short Stocks—Trades Have Been Made Before Consumer Opinions Were Available to Public," *Wall Street Journal*, February 18, 2003.

2. Jon E. Hilsenrath, "Satisfaction Theory: Mixed Yield—Professor's Portfolio Shows Strategy of Linking Returns to Reputation Isn't Perfect," *Wall Street Journal*, February 19, 2003.

3. Ibid.

4. One such is Eugene W. Anderson, Claes Fornell, and Sanal K. Mazvancheryl, "Customer Satisfaction and Shareholder Value," *Journal of Marketing* 68 (October 2004): 172–185.

Chapter 6

1. Random survey of eBay ratings by William F. Reichheld, 2005.

Chapter 7

1. See Julie Creswell, "American Express: Ken Chenault Reshuffles His Cards," *Fortune*, April 5, 2005.

2. *Annual Report to Shareholders, 2004* (Cherry Hill, NJ: Commerce Bancorp Inc., 2004), 4.

Chapter 8

1. Alexandra Kirkman, "Hotel for All Seasons," *Forbes*, October 28, 2002.

ACKNOWLEDGMENTS

I want to thank my colleagues at Bain & Company for continuing to support my obsession with the connection between loyal relationships and economic prosperity. So many Bain partners have helped shape my thinking about loyalty over the years, I cannot list them all here individually. But I do especially want to thank Chris Zook, Jimmy Allen, and Rob Markey for their substantial contributions—both in reading and criticizing early book drafts and in providing material for many of the case studies contained herein. David Bechhofer and Joe Spinelli also made important contributions in translating these ideas into practical applications for Bain clients.

The Bain marketing and editorial staff has also been extremely supportive of my efforts. I am grateful to Wendy Miller, Katie Smith Milway, and Paul Judge for their help not only on this book but on several articles that preceded it.

I have relied heavily on my assistant, Ann Stapleton, to juggle the various responsibilities at Bain as well as speeches, research, and travel. She has done an outstanding job in modulating and prioritizing the never-ending stream of deadlines, requests, and emergencies—reliably and with good humor.

I have received outstanding editorial support in organizing and writing this book. Louise O'Brien helped me through the first phase, turning my jumble of ideas into an organized first draft. Nancy McLaren, my editor for *Loyalty Rules!*, also pitched in on a variety of roles with constant grace and flexibility. For the final draft, I am most thankful to John Case, who demonstrated remarkable craftsmanship and clear thinking. I'm also grateful to Kascha Piotrzkowski and Susan Donovan, who helped to ensure the accuracy of my facts and to prepare the manuscript for publication. Of course, Jeff Kehoe and the entire team at Harvard Business School Press have made substantial contributions throughout the book-creation process. Dave Balter and Michele Hanson of BzzAgent helped all of us determine the best title and have coached me on the creation of electronic communities. In addition to the research funding from Bain & Company, I received vital support from Satmetrix in analyzing which survey questions linked most closely to customer referrals and repurchases. The Satmetrix database of Net Promoter Scores provided a unique resource, without which this book could never have been created. In particular, I want to thank Andre Schwager, Richard Owen, and Laura Brooks for their active support throughout this project. Also, Julian Ting helped us develop the methodology for quantifying the value of word of mouth.

All of the executives who helped me write the case study examples that make up much of this book have been extremely generous with their time. They include Jim Blann (American Express); Diane Hessan (Communispace); Chris Lis (CTCA); Andy Taylor, Sandy Rogers, Dan Gass, and Christy Conrad (Enterprise Rent-A-Car); Isadore Sharp and John Young (Four Seasons); Gary Reiner, Beth Comstock, Chris Moreland, and Pete McCabe (General Electric); Jay Dittman and Tom Brailsford (Hallmark); Jamey Lutz and Pat

Flood (HomeBanc); Tom Kehler (Informative); Scott Cook, Steve Bennett, and Tracy Stevens (Intuit); Ned Bennett (optionsXpress); the late Dave Brumett (SAS); and Feargal Quinn (Superquinn).

I am grateful to Scott Baker, CEO of Paul Davis Restoration, Inc., who provided very helpful feedback on the manuscript from his perspective as an operating executive. I also want to acknowledge the contributions of Jake Barrett, who researched the history of democratic communities.

Finally, I want to thank my entire family for so many dinner-table discussions devoted to companies that succeeded or failed to live up to the Golden Rule principles that are the basis for building quality relationships. I am grateful to my son Billy for his statistical analysis of eBay feedback ratings (and to his high school instructor, Chuck Tiberio, for teaching him the requisite skills). I especially want to thank my wife, Karen, for her patience, love, and support. Her wisdom regarding good relationships and loyalty continues to influence me deeply.

INDEX

accountability
  of a community, 185–187
  of employees for increasing profits,
    16
  granularity of data for, 103–106
  measures for creating, 17
  operational (Enterprise), 66
  opposition to, 182–183
  for responding to feedback, 82
accuracy, auditing for, 106–111
Adelphia, 15
Adobe Systems, 166
advertising, 12, 133
airline industry, 5, 6, 7, 42, 128, 193
  Delta Airlines, 125
  JetBlue Airways, 3, 42, 143
  Southwest Airlines, 3, 7, 10–11, 14,
    42, 91, 178
  US Airways, 7, 178
Allianz, 99
Amazon.com, 10, 19–20, 160–161,
    165–166
American Customer Satisfaction
    Index (ACSI), 83–84, 85
American Express, 99, 124, 130–131,
    133, 178–179
Andrew Harper's Hideaway Report,
    143
anonymity of responders, 101–102
AOL (America Online), 8–9, 11, 13

apology calls, 67
ASDA chain, 42
auditing, ongoing, 112–113
Avis, 119

bad profits
  compared to good, 14–18
  costs of, 4, 9
  customer grid, 120–121
  elimination of (HomeBanc), 46
  good profits versus, 9–14
  reducing, 126–129
  start of, 185
  undermining of growth due to,
    6–9
Bain & Company, 7–8, 15, 42–43, 99,
    117, 180
banking industry, 134–135
Barrett, Colleen, 14, 91
behaviors
  of detractors, 47
  Golden Rule, 13–14, 14–15, 90,
    179–180
  growth-driving, 63
  of promoters, 47
  and responses, links between,
    29–32, 88–89
  validating scores linked to, 112–113
Bennett, Steve, 36, 37. *See also* Intuit
Bezos, Jeff, 10

ABOUT THE AUTHOR

Fred Reichheld is a Director Emeritus of Bain & Company, and in January 1999 was elected the firm's first Bain Fellow. Reichheld joined Bain in 1977 and was elected to the partnership in 1982. His consulting work and research have focused on helping clients achieve superior results through improvements in customer, employee, and partner loyalty. In the June 2003 edition of *Consulting* magazine, Reichheld was included on the list of the world's top twenty-five consultants.

Reichheld's work has been widely covered in the *Wall Street Journal, New York Times, Fortune, BusinessWeek,* and *Economist.* The *Economist* refers to him as the "high priest" of loyalty; the *New York Times* declares, "[He] put loyalty economics on the map." He is the author of eight *Harvard Business Review* articles on the subject, and his two previous books, *The Loyalty Effect* (1996) and *Loyalty Rules!* (2001), were published by Harvard Business School Press. He is a frequent speaker to major business forums and groups of CEOs and senior executives worldwide.

A graduate of Harvard College and Harvard Business School, Mr. Reichheld lives with his wife, Karen, and their family in the Boston area.